THE ELEMENTS OF
USER EXPERIENCE

User-Centered Design for the Web

Jesse James Garrett

American Institue of Graphic Arts
164 Fifth Avenue,
New York, NY 10010

An Imprint of Peachpit,
A Division of Pearson Education
1249 Eighth Street, Berkeley, CA 94710

The Elements of User Experience:
User-Centered Design for the Web

Copyright © 2003 by Jesse James Garrett

International Standard Book Number: 0-7357-1202-6

Library of Congress Catalog Card Number: 2001094557

Printed in the United States of America

First printing: October 2002

15

Trademarks

Warning and Disclaimer

Publisher
David Dwyer

Associate Publisher
Stephanie Wall

Editor in Chief
Chris Nelson

Executive Editor
Steve Weiss

Production Manager
Gina Kanouse

Managing Editor
Sarah Kearns

Acquisitions Editor
Deborah Hittel-Shoaf

Product Marketing Manager
Tammy Detrich

Publicity Manager
Susan Nixon

Project Editor
Jake McFarland

Copy Editor
Amy Lepore

Senior Indexer
Cheryl Lenser

Proofreader
Beth Trudell

Composition
Kim Scott

Manufacturing Coordinator
Jim Conway

Interior Designer
Kim Scott

Cover Designer
Aren Howell

American Institute of Graphic Arts
164 Fifth Avenue
New York, NY 10010
Tel 212 807 1990
Fax 212 807 1799
www.aiga.org

The Elements of User Experience explains, systematically and simply, perhaps the most important development from the confluence of design, technology, and business. Potential should be measured not by what is possible, but how we can adapt the technologically possible to enhance the human experience.

It is not the concept of enhancing a user's experience that is difficult to grasp. It is the challenge of determining how to approach problems while respecting a user's experience. Since the discipline is so young, most young designers have no mentors to turn to. This is where Jesse James Garrett comes in. Garrett has taken this powerful concept and has described clearly how it relates to interaction design through a series of analytic screens that will make both the problem and the solution easier to grasp.

Richard Grefé
Executive director, AIGA

AIGA copublishes selected works by thought leaders in design—authors whose works define new boundaries of design or support practicing designers in their quest for expanding dimensions of excellence and relevance. AIGA is the largest and oldest professional association of designers in the United States. Its members include all disciplines involved in the process of designing.

Dedication

For my wife, who makes all things possible.

Table of Contents

About the Author

Jesse James Garrett is one of the founders of Adaptive Path, a user experience consultancy based in San Francisco. Since 1995, Jesse has worked on Web projects for companies such as AT&T, Intel, Boeing, Motorola, Hewlett-Packard, and National Public Radio. His contributions to the field of user experience include the Visual Vocabulary, an open notation system for information architecture documentation that is now used by organizations around the world. His personal site at **www.jjg.net** is one of the Web's most popular destinations for information architecture resources, and he is a frequent speaker on information architecture and user experience issues.

About the Technical Reviewers

These reviewers contributed their considerable hands-on expertise to the entire development process for *The Elements of User Experience*. As the book was being written, these dedicated professionals reviewed all the material for technical content, organization, and flow. Their feedback was critical to ensuring that *The Elements of User Experience* fits our reader's need for the highest-quality technical information.

David Hoffer has extensive experience in the fields of information architecture and interface design. Currently the senior user interface designer for CTB/McGraw Hill's marketing and communications division, David oversees architecture, interface, and usability. Prior to joining McGraw Hill, David served as a senior information architect for Hill and Knowlton Public Relations—one of the largest U.S. PR firms and part of the second-largest global advertising conglomerate, the WPP Group. David spent two years as senior designer at Amazon.com's Alexa Internet Division, where he developed client interfaces for Amazon's Alexa browser products. David has consulted for a wide range of high-tech firms, including small startups such as NERDS and ActiveBuddy, as well as some of the industry's larger, more-well-known companies such as Motorola and DEC. David holds a B.A. in industrial design from Rochester Institute of Technology, and he hasn't met a dog he doesn't like.

Molly Wright Steenson started working with the Internet in 1994. Since then, she's led the development and architecture of over 60 sites for such companies as Netscape, Reuters, Wrigley, Nike, and Genentech, to name a few. She writes frequently about Internet and design-related issues, and she speaks at conferences internationally. Molly champions a user-centered approach to design and development, and she serves as the AIGA Experience Design site editor. She is a project manager with Razorfish in San Francisco, the proprietress of Girlwonder.com, and fluent in German, French, and Dutch.

Acknowledgments

Don't let the number of names on the cover fool you—it takes a lot of people to make a book happen.

First, I have to thank my partners at Adaptive Path: Lane Becker, Janice Fraser, Mike Kuniavsky, Peter Merholz, Jeffrey Veen, and Indi Young. It is through their indulgence that I was able to take on this project at all.

Then there's everyone at New Riders, particularly Michael Nolan, Karen Whitehouse, Victoria Elzey, Deborah Hittel-Shoaf, John Rahm, and Jake McFarland. Their guidance was essential to this process.

Kim Scott and Aren Howell lent a keen eye and attention to detail to the design of this book. Their patience with suggestions from the author was especially laudable.

Molly Wright Steenson and David Hoffer provided invaluable insight in their review of my manuscript. Every author should be so lucky.

Jess McMullin turned out to be my toughest critic in many ways, and this book is immeasurably improved by his influence.

Thanks are also due to the more experienced authors who gave me advice on how to tackle a project like this and maintain my sanity: Jeffrey Veen (again), Mike Kuniavsky (again), Steve Krug, June Cohen, Nathan Shedroff, Louis Rosenfeld, Peter Morville, and (especially) Steve Champeon.

Others who offered valuable suggestions or simply good moral support included Lisa Chan, George Olsen, Christina Wodtke, Jessamyn West, Samantha Bailey, Eric Scheid, Michael Angeles, Javier Velasco, Antonio Volpon, Vuk Cosic, Thierry Goulet, and Dennis Woudt. They thought of things I didn't, and that makes them the best kind of colleagues.

Musical accompaniment for the writing process was provided by Man or Astro-man?, Pell Mell, Mermen, Dirty Three, Trans Am, Tortoise, Turing Machine, Don Caballero, Mogwai, Ui, Shadowy Men on a Shadowy Planet, Do Make Say Think, and (especially) Godspeed You Black Emperor!

Finally, there are three people without whom this book would never have happened: Dinah Sanders, who at a party one warm Texas night insisted there was someone I had to meet; my wife, Rebecca Blood, who makes me stronger and wiser in every way; and Daniel Grassam, without whose friendship, encouragement, and support I might not have found my way into this business at all. Thank you.

Tell Us What You Think

As the reader of this book, you are the most important critic and commentator. We value your opinion and want to know what we're doing right, what we could do better, what areas you'd like to see us publish in, and any other words of wisdom you're willing to pass our way.

When you contact us, please be sure to include this book's title, ISBN, and author, as well as your name and email address. We will carefully review your comments and share them with the author and editors who worked on the book.

Email: **errata@newriders.com**

Introduction

This is not a how-to book. There are many, many books out there that explain how Web sites get made. This is not one of them.

This is not a book about technology. There is not a single line of code to be found between these covers.

This is not a book of answers. Instead, this book is about asking the right questions.

This book will tell you what you need to know before you go read those other books. If you need the big picture, if you need to understand the context for the decisions that user experience practitioners make, this book is for you.

This book is designed to be read easily in just a few hours. If you're a newcomer to the world of user experience—maybe you're an executive responsible for hiring a user experience team, or maybe you're a writer or designer just finding your way into this field—this book will give you the foundation you need. If you're already familiar with the methods and concerns of the field of user experience, this book will help you communicate them more effectively to the people you work with.

The Story Behind the Book

Because I get asked about it a lot, here is the story of how *The Elements of User Experience* came to be.

In late 1999, I became the first information architect hired into a long-established Web design consultancy. In many ways, I was responsible for defining my position and educating people both about what I did, and how it fit in with what they did. Initially, they were perhaps cautious and a bit wary, but soon they came to recognize that I was there to make their jobs easier, not harder, and that my presence did not mean their authority was diminished.

Simultaneously, I was compiling a personal collection of online material related to my work. (This would eventually find its way onto the Web as my information architecture resources page at **www.jjg.net/ia/**.) While I was doing this research, I was continually frustrated by the seemingly arbitrary and random use of different terms for the basic concepts in the field. What one source called "information design" appeared to be the same as what another called "information architecture." A third rolled everything together under "interface design."

Over the course of late 1999 and January 2000, I struggled to arrive at a self-consistent set of definitions for these concerns and to find a way to express the relationships between them. But I was busy with actual paying work as well, and the model I was trying to formulate wasn't really working out anyway; so by the end of January I had given up on the whole idea.

That March I traveled to Austin, Texas, for the annual South by Southwest Interactive Festival. It was an engaging and thought-provoking week during which I didn't get much sleep—the conference's schedule of day and night activities begins to resemble a marathon after a couple of days.

At the end of that week, as I walked through the terminal of the airport in Austin preparing to board the plane back to San Francisco, it abruptly popped into my head: a three-dimensional matrix that captured all of my ideas. I waited patiently until we boarded the plane. As soon as I reached my seat, I pulled out a notebook and sketched it all out.

Upon my return to San Francisco, I was almost immediately laid up with an enervating head cold. I spent about a week sliding in and out of a fevered delirium. When I felt particularly lucid, I worked on turning my notebook sketch into a finished diagram that would fit neatly onto a letter-size piece of paper. I called it "The Elements of User Experience." Later I would hear about how, for many people, that title evoked memories of periodic tables and Strunk and White. Unfortunately, none of these associations was in my mind when I chose that title—I chose "elements" out of a thesaurus to replace the more awkward and technical-sounding "components."

On March 30, I posted the final product on the Web. (It's still there; you can find the original diagram at **www.jjg.net/ia/elements.pdf**.) The diagram started getting some attention, first from Peter Merholz and Jeffrey Veen, who would later become my partners in Adaptive Path. Soon after, I spoke with more people about it at the first Information Architecture Summit. Eventually I started hearing from people all over the world about how they had used the diagram to educate their co-workers and to give their organizations a common vocabulary for discussing these issues.

In the year after it was first released, "The Elements of User Experience" was downloaded from my site more than 20,000 times. I began to hear about how it was being used in large organizations and tiny Web development groups to help them work and communicate more effectively. By this time, I was beginning to formulate the idea for a book that would address this need better than a single sheet of paper could.

Another March rolled around, and again I found myself in Austin for South by Southwest. There I met Michael Nolan of New Riders Publishing and told him my idea. He was enthusiastic about it, and fortunately, his bosses turned out to be as well.

Thus, as much by luck as by intent, this book found its way into your hands. I hope that what you do with the ideas presented here is as enlightening and rewarding for you as putting them together in this book has been for me.

Jesse James Garrett
July 2002
www.jjg.net/elements/

chapter 1

User Experience and Why It Matters

Technology has been a part of our everyday environment for generations. It empowers us and frustrates us; it simplifies and complicates our lives; it separates us and brings us closer together. But even though we interact with technology every day, we easily forget that technology products are made by people, and that someone, somewhere should get the credit when technology works well for us—or get the blame when it doesn't.

Everyday Miseries

Everyone, every once in a while, has one of those days.

You know the kind of day I'm talking about: You wake up to sunlight streaming in your window and wonder why your alarm clock hasn't gone off yet. You look over to see that your clock thinks it's 3:43 a.m. You stumble out of bed to find another clock, which tells you that you can still make it to work on time—if you leave in 10 minutes.

You turn on the coffeemaker and hustle to get dressed, but when you go to retrieve your dose of life-sustaining caffeine, there's no coffee in the pot. No time to figure out why—you've got to get to work!

You get about a block from your house when you realize that the car needs gas. At the gas station, you try to use the one pump that takes ATM cards, but this time it won't accept your card. So you have to go inside and pay the cashier, but first you have to wait in a line while the cashier very slowly helps everyone in front of you. Finally, you pump your gas and leave the station—to the sound of your gas cap tumbling off the roof of your car and bouncing out into the street.

You have to take a detour because of a traffic accident, so the drive to work takes longer than you expected. It's official: Despite all your efforts, you are now late for work. Finally, you make it to your desk. You're agitated, harried, weary, and irritable—and your day hasn't even really started yet. And you still haven't had any coffee.

Introducing User Experience

It seems like a string of bad luck—just one of those days. But let's look closer and see if, somehow, all that bad luck could have been avoided:

The accident: The accident on the road happened because the driver took his eyes off the road for a moment to turn the radio down. He had to look down because it was impossible to identify which was the volume control by touch alone.

The cap: You lost your gas cap because you set it down on the roof of the car when you started to pump, but then you forgot it because you were feeling rushed. If the cap didn't need to be set down somewhere at all—if it were simply tethered to the car in some way—you couldn't have lost it.

The register: The line at the register in the gas station moved so slowly because the cash register was complex and confusing, and unless the clerk paid extra-close attention while ringing something up, he would make a mistake and have to start all over again. If the register had been simpler and the layout and colors of the buttons different, that line never would have formed.

The pump: You wouldn't have had to stand in that line at all if the pump had accepted your ATM card. It would have done so if you had turned the card around the other way, but nothing on the pump indicated which way the card should be turned, and you were in such a hurry that you didn't think to try every orientation.

The coffeemaker: The coffeemaker didn't make coffee because you didn't push down the On button all the way. The machine doesn't do anything to let you know that it has been turned on: no light, no sound, no little "click" when the button makes contact. You thought you had turned it on, but you were wrong. The problem could have been avoided altogether if you had set the coffeemaker to start brewing automatically first thing in the morning, but you never learned how to use that function—if you knew it existed at all.

The clock: And then, we come to the factor that started the whole chain of events—the alarm clock. The alarm didn't go off because the time was wrong. The time was wrong because your cat stepped on the clock in the middle of the night and reset it for you. (If this sounds implausible to you, don't laugh—it has happened to me. I have had to go to surprising lengths to find a clock that is impervious to cat meddling.) A slightly different configuration of buttons would have prevented the cat from resetting the clock, and consequently you would have been out of bed with plenty of time—no need to rush at all.

In short, every one of the previous incidents of "bad luck" could have been avoided had someone taken more care in designing a product. These examples all demonstrate a lack of attention to the **user experience**: how the product behaves and is used in the real world. When a product is being developed, people pay a great deal of attention to what it does. User experience is the other, often overlooked, side of the equation—how it works—that can often make the difference between a successful product and a failure.

User experience is not about how a product works on the inside (although that sometimes has a lot of influence). User experience is about how it works on the outside, where a person comes into contact with it and has to work with it. That interaction often involves pushing a lot of buttons, as in the case of technology products such as alarm clocks, coffeemakers, or cash registers. Sometimes, it's just a matter of a simple physical mechanism, such as the gas cap on your car. However, every product that is used by someone has a user experience: newspapers, ketchup bottles, reclining armchairs, cardigan sweaters.

No matter what kind of product is involved, it's the little things that count. Having a button click when you push it down doesn't seem like much, but when that click makes the difference between getting coffee and not getting coffee, it matters a great deal. Even if you never realized that the design of that button was causing you trouble, how would you feel about a coffeemaker that you were able to use successfully only part of the time? How would you feel about the manufacturer? Would you buy another product from that company in the future? Probably not. Thus, for the want of a button that clicks, a customer is lost.

User Experience and the Web

This book is about the user experience of one particular kind of product: Web sites. On the Web, user experience becomes even more important than it is for other kinds of products.

In virtually every case, a Web site is a "self-service" product. There is no instruction manual to read beforehand, no training seminar to attend, no customer service representative to help guide the user through the site. There is only the user, facing the site alone with only her wits and experience to guide her.

It's bad enough that she's been stuck in the position of having to figure out the site on her own. The fact that most sites don't even acknowledge this only makes matters worse. Despite the vital strategic importance of user experience to the success of a Web site, the simple matter of understanding what people want and need has been a low priority for most of the history of the Web.

Faced with a wide array of choices, the user is left to her own devices to determine which features of a site will meet her needs.

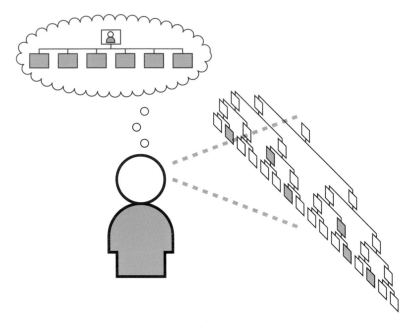

How did this come to pass? In the earliest days of the Web, many thought being first to market was the key to success. Sites like Yahoo! built early leads that later competitors struggled to overcome. Established companies raced to set up Web sites, determined not to be perceived as falling behind the times. But in most cases, companies considered merely having deployed the site a great accomplishment; whether the site actually worked for people was, at best, an afterthought.

To gain market share against these "first-mover" sites, competitors began to emphasize features, adding more and more content and functionality to their sites in hopes of drawing in those who were new to the Web (and maybe stealing a few customers from the competition).

Having more features, however, turned out to be only a temporary source of competitive advantage. With the added complexity that came with an ever-expanding feature set, sites became increasingly unwieldy, hard to use, and unappealing to the very first-timers they were supposed to draw in. And still, many organizations paid little attention to what actual users liked, found valuable, or were really able to use.

Businesses have now come to recognize that providing a quality user experience is an essential, sustainable competitive advantage. It is user experience that forms the customer's impression of the company's offerings, it is user experience that differentiates the company from its competitors, and it is user experience that determines whether your customer will ever come back.

Competitive Advantage and ROI

Maybe you don't sell anything on your site. All you provide is information about your company. It might seem that you have a monopoly on that information—if people want it, they have to get it from you. You don't have competition in the same way that an online bookstore does. Nevertheless, you can't afford to neglect the user experience of your site.

If your site consists mainly of what we Web types call "content"— that is, information—then one of the main goals of your site is to communicate that information as effectively as possible. It's not enough just to put it out there. It has to be presented in a way that helps people absorb it and understand it. Otherwise, the user might not ever find out that you offer the service or product they're looking for. And even if they do manage to find that information, they're likely to draw the conclusion that if your site is difficult to work with, you probably are as well.

Even if your site mostly comprises interactive tools that people can use to accomplish certain tasks (like buying airplane tickets or managing bank accounts), effective communication is a key factor in the success of your product. The world's most powerful functionality will falter and fail if users can't figure out how to make it work.

Simply put, if your users have a bad experience, they won't come back. If they have an okay experience with your site but a better experience with your competitor's site, they'll go back to that competitor, not you. Features and functions always matter, but user experience has a far greater effect on customer loyalty. All your sophisticated technology and corporate messaging won't bring those customers back a second time. A good user experience will—and you don't get much of a second chance to get it right.

Customer loyalty isn't the only way that focusing on the user experience of your site can pay off. Businesses with an eye on the bottom line want to know about the **return on investment**, or ROI. ROI is usually measured in terms of money: For every dollar you spend, how many dollars of value are you getting back? That's the ROI. But return on investment does not have to be expressed in strictly monetary terms. All you need is a measurement that shows that your money going out translates into value for your company.

One common measure of return on investment is **conversion rate**. Any time you want to encourage your customers to take the next step in building a relationship with you—whether that involves something as complex as customizing the site to their preferences or as simple as signing up to receive an e-mail newsletter—there's a conversion rate you can measure. By keeping track of what percentage of users you "convert" to the next level, you can measure how effectively your site is meeting your business goals.

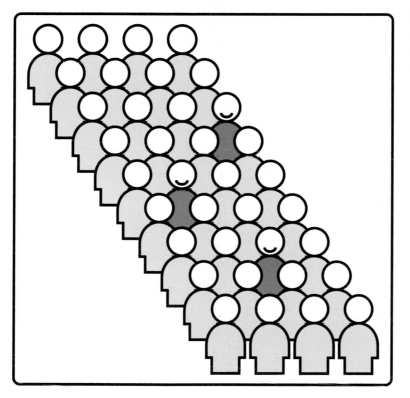

Conversion rate is a common way of measuring the effectiveness of a user experience.

3 subscription sign-ups

÷

36 visitors

=

8.33% conversion rate

Conversion rate becomes even more important in the case of commerce sites. Far more people browse a commerce site than buy from it. A quality user experience is a key factor in "converting" these casual browsers into active buyers. Even a tiny increase in your conversion rate can translate into a dramatic leap in revenue. It's not uncommon for a change in conversion rate of only one-tenth of one percent to result in a revenue increase of ten percent or more.

On any site where users have the opportunity to give you some money, you have a conversion rate you can measure, whether you're selling books, cat food, or subscriptions to the content of the site itself. Conversion rate can give you a better sense of the return on your user experience investment than simple sales figures. Sales can suffer if you're not successful in getting the word out about your site. Conversion rate tracks how successful you are in getting those who visit to spend some money.

A related measure of user experience ROI for commerce sites is the incidence of abandoned shopping carts. Putting items in a cart indicates a willingness to make a purchase, but all too frequently those carts simply languish because the purchase process itself was too difficult, confusing, or time-consuming. As with conversion rate, refinements to the user experience can reduce the incidence of abandoned carts.

Even if your site doesn't lend itself readily to ROI measures like these, it doesn't mean the effect of user experience on your business is any less significant. Whether they are used by your customers, your partners, or your employees, Web sites can have all kinds of indirect effects on the bottom line.

Web sites are complicated pieces of technology, and something
funny happens when people have trouble using complicated pieces
of technology: they blame themselves. They feel like they must have
done something wrong. They feel like they weren't paying enough
attention. They feel stupid. Sure, it's irrational. After all, it's not their
fault the site doesn't work the way they expect it to. But they feel
stupid anyway. And if you intend to drive people away from your
site, it's hard to imagine a more effective approach than making
them feel stupid when they use it.

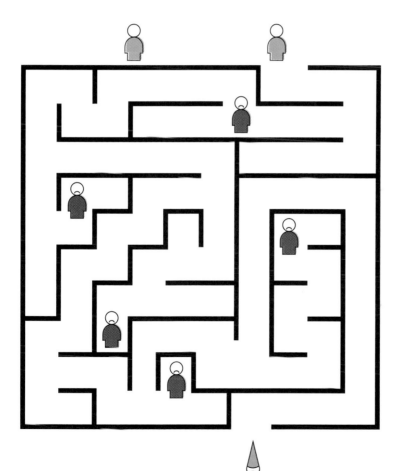

Technology products
that don't work the way
people expect make
them feel stupid—even
if they actually accom-
plished what they set
out to do.

No one outside your company might ever see your site (as in the case of an intranet), but the user experience still makes a huge difference. Often, it can mean the difference between a project that creates value for the organization and a project that becomes a resource-consuming nightmare.

Any user experience effort aims to improve efficiency. This basically comes in two key forms: helping people work faster and helping them make fewer mistakes. Improving the efficiency of the tools you use improves the productivity of the business as a whole. The less time it takes to complete any given task, the more you can get done in a day. In keeping with the old notion that time is money, saving your employees time translates directly into saving your business money.

Efficiency doesn't only affect the bottom line, though. People like their jobs more when their tools are natural and easy to use, not frustrating and needlessly complex. If that person is you, these kinds of tools make the difference between coming home at the end of the day satisfied and coming home exhausted. (Or at least, if you are coming home exhausted, it's for the right reasons, not because you've been struggling with your tools.)

If that person is your employee, providing these kinds of tools increases not only their productivity, but also their job satisfaction, making the employee less likely to seek a new job. This, in turn, means you save on recruiting and training costs, plus you benefit from the higher level of quality that a more dedicated, experienced employee brings to the work she does.

Minding Your Users

The practice of creating engaging, efficient user experiences is called **user-centered design**. The concept of user-centered design is very simple: Every step of the way, take the user into account as you develop your product. The implications of this simple concept, however, are surprisingly complex.

Everything the user experiences should be the result of a conscious decision on your part. Realistically, you might have to make a compromise here and there because of the time or expense involved in creating a better solution. But a user-centered design process ensures that those compromises don't happen by accident. By thinking about the user experience, breaking it down into its component elements, and looking at it from several perspectives, you can ensure that you know all the ramifications of your decisions.

The biggest reason user experience should matter to you is that it matters to your users. If you don't provide them with a positive experience, they won't use your site. And without users, all you've got is a dusty Web server somewhere, idly waiting to fulfill a request that will never come. For the users who do come, you must set out to provide them with an experience that is coherent, intuitive, and maybe even pleasurable—an experience in which everything works the way it should. No matter how the rest of their day has gone.

chapter **2**

Meet the
Elements

The user experience development process is all about ensuring that no aspect of the user's experience with your site happens without your conscious, explicit intent. This means taking into account every possibility of every action the user is likely to take and understanding the user's expectations at every step of the way through that process. It sounds like a big job, and in some ways it is. But by breaking the job of crafting user experience down into its component elements, we can better understand the problem as a whole.

The Five Planes

Most people, at one time or another, have purchased a book over the Web. The experience is pretty much the same every time—you go to the site, you find the book you want (maybe by using a search engine or maybe by browsing a catalog), you give the site your credit card number and your address, and the site confirms that the book will be shipped to you.

That neat, tidy experience actually results from a whole set of decisions—some small, some large—about how the site looks, how it behaves, and what it allows you to do. These decisions build upon each other, informing and influencing all aspects of the user experience. If we peel away the layers of that experience, we can begin to understand how those decisions are made.

The Surface Plane

On the **surface** you see a series of Web pages, made up of images and text. Some of these images are things you can click on, performing some sort of function such as taking you to a shopping cart. Some of these images are just illustrations, such as a photograph of a book cover or the logo of the site itself.

The Skeleton Plane

Beneath that surface is the **skeleton** of the site: the placement of buttons, tabs, photos, and blocks of text. The skeleton is designed to optimize the arrangement of these elements for maximum effect and efficiency—so that you remember the logo and can find that shopping cart button when you need it.

The Structure Plane

The skeleton is a concrete expression of the more abstract **structure** of the site. The skeleton might define the placement of the interface elements on our checkout page; the structure would define how users got to that page and where they could go when they were finished there. The skeleton might define the arrangement of navigational items allowing the users to browse categories of books; the structure would define what those categories actually were.

The Scope Plane

The structure defines the way in which the various features and functions of the site fit together. Just what those features and functions are constitutes the **scope** of the site. Some sites that sell books offer a feature that enables users to save previously used addresses so they can be used again. The question of whether that feature—or any feature—is included on a site is a question of scope.

The Strategy Plane

The scope is fundamentally determined by the **strategy** of the site. This strategy incorporates not only what the people running the site want to get out of it but what the users want to get out of the site as well. In the case of our bookstore example, some of the strategic objectives are pretty obvious: Users want to buy books, and we want to sell them. Other objectives might not be so easy to articulate.

Building from Bottom to Top

These five planes—strategy, scope, structure, skeleton, and surface—provide a conceptual framework for talking about user experience problems and the tools we use to solve them.

On each plane, the issues we must deal with become a little less abstract and a little more concrete. On the lowest plane, we are not concerned with the final shape of the site at all—we only care about how the site will fit into our strategy (while meeting the needs of our users). On the highest plane, we are only concerned with the most concrete details of the appearance of the site. Plane by plane, the decisions we have to make become a little more specific and involve finer levels of detail.

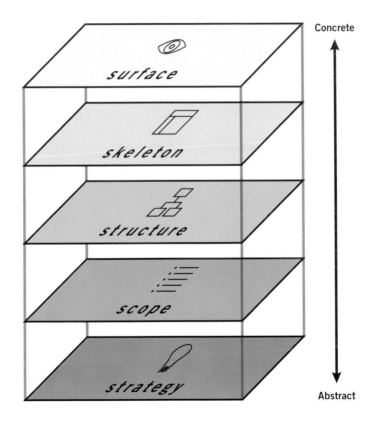

Each plane is dependent on the planes below it. So, the surface depends on the skeleton, which depends on the structure, which depends on the scope, which depends on the strategy. When the choices we make don't align with those above and below, projects often derail, deadlines are missed, and costs begin to skyrocket as the development team tries to piece together components that don't naturally fit. Even worse, when the site finally does launch, the users will hate it. This dependence means that decisions on the strategy plane will have a sort of "ripple effect" all the way up the chain. Conversely, the choices available to us on each plane are constrained by the decisions we make about issues on the planes below it.

range of choices available on the next plane

the option you chose

range of possible choices

The choices you make on each plane affect the choices available to you on the next plane above it.

This ripple effect means that choosing an "out of bounds" option on an upper plane will require rethinking decisions on lower planes.

That does not mean, however, that every decision about the lower plane must be made before the upper plane can be addressed. Dependencies run in both directions, with decisions made on upper planes sometimes forcing a reevaluation (or an evaluation made for the first time!) of decisions on lower planes. At each level, we make decisions according to what the competition is doing, industry best practices, and plain old common sense. These decisions can have a ripple effect in both directions.

If you consider your decisions on lower planes to be set in stone before you take on your decisions on higher planes, you will almost certainly be throwing your project schedule at the very least—and possibly the success of your final product—into jeopardy.

Instead, you should plan your project so that work on any plane cannot *finish* before work on lower planes has finished. The important consideration here is not to build the roof of the house before we know the shape of its foundation.

Requiring work on each plane to **finish** before work on the next can **start** leads to unsatisfactory results for you and your users.

A better approach is to have work on each plane **finish** before work on the next can **finish**.

A Basic Duality

Of course, there are more than just five elements of user experience, and as with any specialized field, this one has evolved a vocabulary all its own. To someone encountering the field for the first time, user experience can appear to be a complicated business. All these seemingly identical terms are thrown around: interaction design, information design, information architecture. What do they mean? Anything? Or are they just more meaningless industry buzzwords?

To further complicate matters, people will use the same terms in different ways. One person might use "information design" to refer to what another knows as "information architecture." And what's the difference between "interface design" and "interaction design?" Is there one?

Fortunately, the field of user experience seems to be moving out of this Babel-like state. Consistency is gradually creeping into our discussions of these issues. To understand the terms themselves, however, we should look at where they came from.

When the Web started, it was just about hypertext. People could create documents, and they could link them to other documents. Tim Berners-Lee, the inventor of the Web, created it as a way for researchers in the high-energy physics community, who were spread out all over the world, to share and refer to each other's findings. He knew the Web had the potential to be much more than that, but few others really understood how great its potential was.

People originally seized on the Web as a new publishing medium, but as technology advanced and new features were added to Web browsers and Web servers alike, the Web took on new capabilities. After the Web began to catch on in the larger Internet community, it developed a more complex and robust feature set that would enable Web sites not only to distribute information but to collect and manipulate it as well. With this, the Web became more interactive, responding to the input of users in ways that were very much like traditional desktop applications.

With the advent of commercial interests on the Web, this application functionality found a wide range of uses, such as electronic commerce, community forums, and online banking, among others. Meanwhile, the Web continued to flourish as a publishing medium, with countless newspaper and magazine sites augmenting the wave of Web-only "e-zines" being published. Technology continued to advance on both fronts as all kinds of sites made the transition from static collections of information that changed infrequently to dynamic, database-driven sites that were constantly evolving.

When the Web user experience community started to form, its members spoke two different languages. One group saw every problem as an application design problem, and applied problem-solving approaches from the traditional desktop and mainframe software worlds. (These, in turn, were rooted in common practices applied to creating all kinds of products, from cars to running shoes.) The other group saw the Web in terms of information distribution and retrieval, and applied problem-solving approaches from the traditional worlds of publishing, media, and information science.

This became quite a stumbling block. Very little progress could be made when the community could not even agree on basic terminology. The waters were further muddied by the fact that many Web sites could not be neatly categorized as either applications or hypertext information spaces—a huge number seemed to be a sort of hybrid, incorporating qualities from each world.

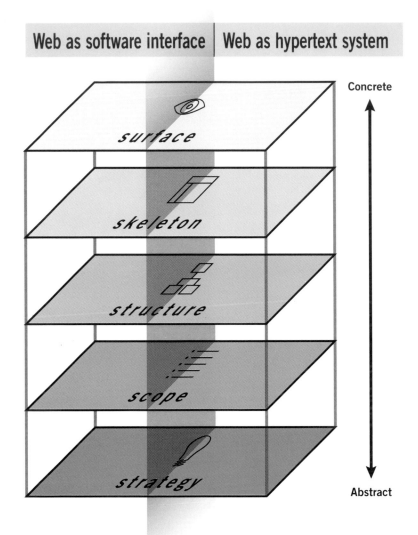

To address this basic duality in the nature of the Web, let's split our five planes down the middle. On the left, we'll put those elements specific to using the Web as a **software interface**. On the right, we'll put the elements specific to **hypertext information spaces**.

On the software side, we are mainly concerned with **tasks**—the steps involved in a process and how people think about completing them. Here, we consider the site as a tool or set of tools that the user employs to accomplish one or more tasks.

On the hypertext side, our concern is **information**—what information the site offers and what it means to our users. Hypertext is about creating an information space that users can move through.

The Elements of User Experience

Now we can map that whole confusing array of terms into the model. By breaking each plane down into its component elements, we'll be able to take a closer look at how all the pieces fit together to create the whole user experience.

The Strategy Plane

The same strategic concerns come into play for both software products and information spaces. **User needs** are the goals for the site that come from outside our organization—specifically from the people who will use our site. We must understand what our audience wants from us and how that fits in with other goals it has.

Balanced against user needs are our own objectives for the site. These **site objectives** can be business goals ("Make $1 million in sales over the Web this year") or other kinds of goals ("Inform voters about the candidates in the next election"). In Chapter 3 we'll go into more detail about these elements.

The Scope Plane

On the software side, the strategy is translated into scope through the creation of **functional specifications**: a detailed description of the "feature set" of the product. On the information space side, scope takes the form of **content requirements**: a description of the various content elements that will be required. Chapter 4 will cover the scope elements.

The Structure Plane

The scope is given structure on the software side through **interaction design**, in which we define how the system behaves in response to the user. For information spaces, the structure is the **information architecture**: the arrangement of content elements within the information space. You'll find more details on these in Chapter 5.

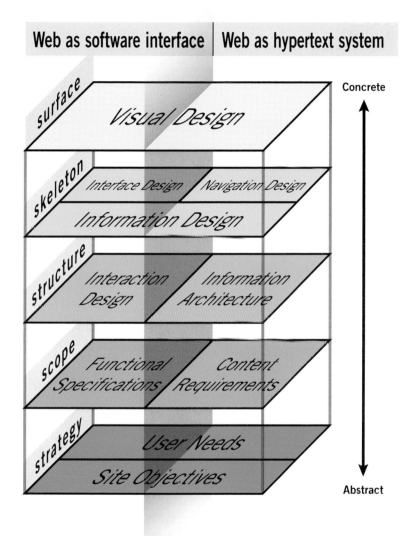

The Skeleton Plane

The skeleton plane breaks down into three components. On both sides, we must address **information design**: the presentation of information in a way that facilitates understanding. For software products, the skeleton also includes **interface design**, or arranging interface elements to enable users to interact with the functionality of the system. The interface for an information space is its **navigation design**: the set of screen elements that allow the user to move through the information architecture. There's more about the skeleton plane in Chapter 6.

The Surface Plane

Finally, we have the surface. Regardless of whether we are dealing with a software product or an information space, our concern here is the same: the **visual design**, or the look of the finished product. It's trickier than it sounds; you can find out all about it in Chapter 7.

Using the Elements

Few sites fall exclusively on one side of this model or the other. Within each plane, the elements must work together to accomplish that plane's goals. For example, information design, navigation design, and interface design jointly define the skeleton of a site. The effects of decisions you make about one element from all other elements on the plane is very difficult. All the elements on every plane have a common function—in this example, defining the site's skeleton—even if they perform that function in different ways.

This model, divided up into neat boxes and planes, is a convenient way to think about user experience problems. In reality, however, the lines between these areas are not so clearly drawn. Frequently, it can be difficult to identify whether a particular user experience problem is best solved through attention to one element instead of another. Can a change to the visual design do the trick, or will the underlying navigation design have to be reworked? Some problems require attention in several areas at once, and some seem to straddle the borders identified in this model.

The way organizations often delegate responsibility for user experience issues only complicates matters further. In some organizations, you will encounter people with job titles like information architect or interface designer. Don't be confused by this. These people generally have expertise spanning many of the elements of user experience, not just the specialty indicated by their title. It's not necessary to have a member of your team who is a specialist in each of these areas; instead, you only have to ensure that someone is responsible for thinking about each of these issues.

A couple of additional factors go into shaping the final user experience that you won't find covered in detail here. The first of these is **content**. The old saying (well, old in Web years) is that "content is king" on the Web. This is absolutely true—the single most important thing most Web sites can offer to their users is content that those users will find valuable.

Users don't visit Web sites to experience the joy of navigation. The content that is available to you (or that you have resources to obtain and manage) will play a huge role in shaping your site. In the case of our bookstore site example, we might decide that we want the users to be able to see cover images of all the books we sell. If we can get them, will we have a way to catalog them, keep track of them, and keep them up to date? And what if we can't get photos of the book covers at all? These content questions are essential to the ultimate user experience of the site.

Second, **technology** can be just as important as content in creating a successful user experience. In many cases, the nature of the experience you can provide your users is largely determined by technology. In the early days of the Web, the tools to connect Web sites to databases were fairly primitive and limited. As the technology has advanced, however, databases have become more widely used to drive Web sites. This in turn has enabled more and more sophisticated user experience approaches, such as dynamic navigation systems that change in response to the way users move through the site. Technology is always changing, and the field of user experience always has to adapt to it. Nevertheless, the fundamental elements of user experience remain the same.

The rest of this book looks at the elements, plane by plane, in greater detail. We'll take a closer look at some of the tools and techniques commonly used to address each element. We'll see what the elements on each plane have in common, what makes each one different, and how they affect each other to create the total user experience.

chapter **3**

The Strategy Plane

Site Objectives and User Needs

The foundation of a successful user experience is a clearly articulated strategy. Knowing both what we want the site to accomplish for our organization and what we want the site to accomplish for our users helps inform all the decisions we have to make about every aspect of the user experience. But answering these simple questions can be trickier than it looks.

Surface

Skeleton

Structure

Scope

Strategy

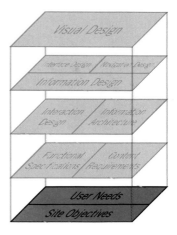

Defining the Strategy

The most common reason for the failure of a Web site is not technology. It's not user experience either. Web sites most often fail because, before the first line of code was written, the first pixel was pushed, or the first server was installed, nobody bothered to answer two very basic questions:

▶ What do we want to get out of this site?

▶ What do our users want to get out of it?

By answering the first question, we describe the **site objectives** coming from inside the organization. The second question addresses **user needs**, objectives imposed on the site from outside. Together, site objectives and user needs form the strategy plane, the foundation for every decision in our process as we design the user experience. Yet, amazingly, many user experience projects do not begin with a clear, explicit understanding of the underlying strategy.

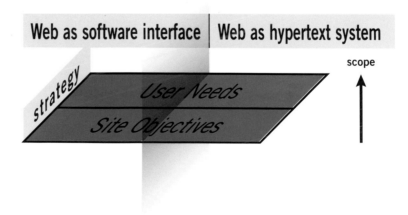

The key word here is *explicit*. The more clearly we can articulate exactly what we want, and exactly what others want from us, the more precisely we can adjust the choices we make to meet these goals.

Site Objectives

The first part of making our understanding of the strategy explicit is examining our own objectives for the site. Too often, site objectives exist only as an unspoken understanding among those building the site. When that understanding remains unspoken, different people often have different ideas about what the project is supposed to accomplish.

Business Goals

People commonly use terms like "business goals" or "business drivers" to describe internal strategic objectives. I'm going to use the term "site objectives" because I think these other terms are both too narrow and too broad: Too narrow because not every internal goal is a business goal (after all, not every organization has the same kinds of goals that businesses do), and too broad because our concern here really is to identify in the most specific terms possible what we expect the site itself to accomplish, the rest of our activities notwithstanding.

Most people start out describing site objectives in very general terms. At the most fundamental level, business Web sites generally exist to serve one of two purposes: to make the company money or to save the company money. Sometimes it's both. But exactly how these sites are supposed to do that is not always clear.

On the other hand, objectives that are too specific don't adequately describe the strategic concerns at issue. For example, stating that one of your objectives is "to provide users with a Java-based real-time communications tool" doesn't explain how such a tool helps advance the objectives of your organization, or how it helps meet the needs of your users.

In trying to strike a balance between being too specific and being too general, we want to avoid jumping ahead to identify solutions when we don't yet fully understand the problems. To create a successful user experience, we have to make sure that nothing is determined by accident—that every decision we make is rooted in a firm understanding of its consequences.

Brand Identity

One essential consideration in formulating the objectives for any site is brand identity. When most of us see the word "branding," we think of things like logos, color palettes, and typography. While these visual aspects of brand are important (we'll revisit them in more detail when we get to the surface plane in Chapter 7), the concept of brand extends far beyond the visual. Brand identity—a set of conceptual associations or emotional reactions—is important because it's inescapable. In the minds of your users, an impression about your organization is inevitably created by their interaction with your site.

You must choose whether that impression happens by accident or as a result of conscious choices you have made in designing your site. Most organizations choose to exert some control over the perception of their brand, which is why communicating brand identity is a very common site objective. Branding isn't just for commercial entities either—every organization with a Web site, from non-profit foundations to government agencies, creates an impression through user experience. By codifying the specific qualities of that impression as an explicit objective, you increase your chances that it will be a positive impression.

Success Metrics

Races have finish lines. An important part of understanding your objectives is understanding how you will know when you have reached them.

These are known as **success metrics**: indicators we can track after the site has been deployed to see whether it is meeting our own objectives and our users' needs. Good success metrics not only influence decisions made over the course of the project, they also provide concrete evidence of the value of user experience efforts if you find yourself facing a skeptical audience when seeking budget approval for your next user experience project.

Success metrics are concrete indicators of how effectively the user experience is meeting strategic goals. In this example, measuring the number of visits per registered user per month indicates how valuable the site is to its core audience.

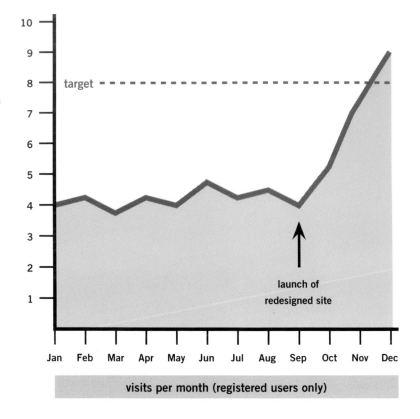

visits per month (registered users only)

Sometimes these metrics are related to the site itself and how it is used. How much time does the average user spend on your site during each visit? (Your server logs can help you determine this.) If you want to encourage your users to feel comfortable with the site, hang out, and explore what you have to offer, you'll want to see the time per visit increase. On the other hand, if you want to provide quick, get-in-get-out access to information and functionality, you may want to decrease the time per visit.

For sites that depend on advertising revenue, page views—the number of times each day a page on your site is requested—is an incredibly important metric. But you have to be careful to balance your objectives and the needs of your users. Adding several layers of navigational pages between the home page and the content users want will definitely increase your page views, but is it serving user needs? Probably not. And in the long run, it will show: as your users get frustrated and decide not to come back, your page views will drop from that initial high and will probably end up lower than they were when you started.

Not all success metrics have to be derived directly from your site. You can measure the indirect effects of the site as well. If your site provides solutions to common problems people encounter with your product, the number of phone calls coming into your customer support lines should go down. An effective intranet can provide ready access to tools and resources that can cut down on the time it takes for your salespeople to close a sale—which, in turn, translates directly into increased revenue.

The metrics that work best are those for which a change can be directly attributed to the user experience of the site. Of course, when a redesign launches and daily revenue from online transactions jumps 40 percent, it's easy to see the relationship between cause and effect. But for changes that happen over a longer period of time, it can be difficult to identify whether those changes stem from the user experience or from other factors.

For example, the user experience of your site can't do much by itself to bring new users to your site—you'll have to rely upon word-of-mouth or your marketing efforts for that. But the user experience has a whole lot of influence on whether those visitors bother to come back. Measuring return visits can be a great way to assess whether you're meeting user needs, but be careful: Sometimes those users don't come back because your competitor launched a gigantic advertising campaign or because your company just got some bad press. Any metric viewed in isolation can be misleading; be sure to take a step back and look at what's going on beyond the Web site to make sure you're getting the whole story.

User Needs

It can be easy to fall into the trap of thinking that we are designing our site for one idealized user—someone exactly like us. But we aren't designing for ourselves; we're designing for other people, and if those other people are going to like and use what we create, we need to understand who they are and what they need. By spending time researching those needs, we can break out of our own limited perspective and see the site from the point of view of the users.

Identifying user needs can be complicated because users can be quite diverse. Even if we're creating a site for use inside our organization, we still may have to address a wide range of needs. If our site is intended for a consumer audience, the possibilities increase exponentially.

User Segmentation

We can break this mass of user needs down into manageable chunks through **user segmentation**. We divide our audience into smaller groups (or segments) consisting of users with certain key character- istics in common. There are nearly as many ways to segment user groups as there are types of users, but here are a couple of the most common approaches.

Market researchers commonly create audience segments based on **demographic** criteria: gender, age, education level, marital status, income, and so on. These demographic profiles can be quite general (men 18–49) or very specific (unmarried, college-educated women 25–34 making over $50,000 a year).

Demographics aren't the only way you can look at your users. **Psychographic** profiles describe the attitudes and perceptions that your users have about the world or about the subject matter of your site in particular. Psychographics often correlate strongly with demo- graphics: People in the same age group, location, and income level often have similar attitudes. Still, documenting the psychographics of your users can give you insights you can't get from demographics.

When developing Web sites, there's another very important set of attitudes to consider: the users' attitudes toward technology and the Web itself. How much time do your users spend using the Web every week? Are computers a part of their daily lives? Do they like work- ing with technology? Do they always have the latest and greatest hardware, or do they only buy a computer every five years? Technophobes and power users approach Web sites in very different ways, and our designs need to accommodate them. Answers to ques- tions like these can help us do just that.

User segmentation
helps us understand
user needs better by
dividing the entire
audience into smaller
groups of people with
shared needs.

In addition to understanding our users' familiarity and comfort level with technology, we need to understand what and how much they know about the subject matter of our site. Selling cookware to people just learning their way around a kitchen must be handled very differently from selling to professional cooks. Similarly, a stock-trading application used by those unfamiliar with the stock market will require a different approach from one for seasoned investors.

The way people use information often depends on their social or professional role. The information needs of the parents of a student applying for college are different from those of the student herself. Identifying the different roles of the users who come to your site can help you separate and analyze their different needs.

After you've conducted some research on your user groups, you might need to revise the segments you are working with. For example, if you're researching 25–34 year old, college-educated women, you might find that the needs of the 30–34 year olds differ from those of the 25–29 age group. If the difference is great enough, you might want to treat these as separate groups, rather than the single 25–34 group above. On the other hand, if the 18–24 group seems pretty similar to the 25–34 group, maybe you can combine them. Creating user segments is just a means to the end of uncovering user needs. You really only need as many different segments as you have different sets of user needs.

There's another important reason to create user segments. Not only will different groups of users have different needs, but sometimes those needs will be in direct opposition. Take the preceding example of the stock-trading application. The novices would probably be best served by an application that broke the process down into a sequence of simple steps. For the experts, however, such a sequence would be a hindrance. The experts need a unified interface that provides rapid access to a wide range of functions.

Obviously, we can't meet both sets of user needs with a single solution. Our options at this point are to focus on one user segment to the exclusion of the other, or to provide two separate ways for users to approach the same task. Whichever course we choose, this strategic decision will have consequences for every additional choice we make about the user experience.

Usability and User Research

If you've done any reading about Web design at all, you've probably come across the word **usability**. The concept means different things to different people. Some people use it to refer to the practice of testing designs with representative users. For others, it means adopting a very specific development methodology. But every approach to usability seeks to make products easier to use.

Many different definitions and lists of rules intend to codify what constitutes a usable Web site design. Some of them even agree with each other. But they all have the same principle at their core: Users need usable products. It's really the most universal user need of all.

To understand what our users need, we first have to get a sense of who they are. The field of **user research** is devoted to collecting the data needed to develop that understanding.

Some research tools—such as surveys, interviews, or focus groups—are best suited for gathering information about the general attitudes and perceptions of your users.

Other research tools—such as user tests or field studies—are more appropriate for understanding specific aspects of user behavior and interaction with the site.

Generally, the more time you spend with each individual user, the more detailed the information you will get from the research study. At the same time, that additional time spent with each user necessarily means you won't be able to include as many users in the study (if only because the site has to launch eventually).

Market research methods like surveys and focus groups can be valuable sources of general information about your users. These methods are most effective when you clearly articulate for yourself what information you're trying to get out of them. Do you want to find out what your users are doing when they use a particular feature of your site? Or maybe you already know that, but you need to know why they're doing it. The more clearly you can describe what you want, the more narrowly and effectively you can formulate the questions you ask to ensure that you get the right information.

Contextual inquiry refers to a whole set of methods that, collectively, form the most powerful and comprehensive toolkit for understanding your users in the *context* of their everyday lives (hence the name). These techniques are derived from the methods used by anthropologists to study cultures and societies. Applied on a smaller scale, the same methods used to examine, for example, how a nomadic tribe functions, can also be used to examine how people who buy aircraft parts function. The only downside is that contextual inquiry can sometimes be very time-consuming and very expensive. But if you have the resources, and your problem requires a deeper understanding of your users, contextual inquiry can reveal subtleties of user behavior that can't be discovered through other methods.

One method closely related to contextual inquiry is **task analysis**. The idea behind task analysis is that every user's interaction with a Web site takes place in the context of some task that user is performing. Sometimes the task is very focused (such as buying movie tickets) and sometimes it's broader (such as learning about international commerce regulations). Task analysis is a method of closely examining the precise steps users go through in accomplishing those tasks. This examination can be done either through interviews in which you get users to tell you stories about their experiences or through direct observation in the field, observing the users in their "natural habitat."

User testing is the most commonly employed form of user research. User testing is not about testing your users; instead, it's about getting your users to test what you've produced. Sometimes user tests work with a finished site, either in preparation for a redesign or to root out any usability issues before launch. In other cases, users can test a work in progress or even a rough prototype of the finished site.

Tests with a fully operational Web site can be very broad or very narrow in scope. As with surveys or focus groups, it's best if you have a clear sense of what you want to investigate before you sit down with users. That doesn't mean, however, that a user test has to be strictly limited to assessing how successfully users complete a narrowly defined task. User testing can also investigate broader, less concrete issues. For example, a user test could be used to find out whether modifications to the site design reinforce or undermine the company's brand message.

Another approach to user testing is to have users work with prototypes. These can take a variety of forms, from rough sketches on paper, to "lo-fi" mockups using stripped-down HTML pages, to "click-through" prototypes that create the illusion of a finished site. Larger-scale projects employ different kinds of prototypes at different stages to gather user input all the way through the development process.

Sometimes user tests don't involve the site at all. You can recruit users to perform a variety of different exercises that can give you insights into how they approach the subject matter of your site. **Card sorting** is one method used to explore how users categorize or group information elements. The user is given a stack of index cards, each of which has the name, description, or image of a piece or type of content on it. The user then sorts the cards into piles according to the groups or categories that feel most natural. Analyzing the results of card sorts conducted with several users can help us understand how they think about the information our site provides.

Collecting all sorts of data about your users can be incredibly valuable, but sometimes you can lose sight of the real people behind all the statistics. You can make your users more real by turning them into **personas** (sometimes called *user models* or *user profiles*). A persona is a fictional character constructed to represent the needs of a whole range of real users. By putting a face and a name on the disconnected bits of data from your user research and segmentation work, personas can help ensure that you keep the users in mind during the design process.

Let's look at an example. Suppose our site is designed to provide information for people who are starting their own businesses. We know from our research that our audience mostly falls in the 30–45 age range. Our users tend to be fairly comfortable with the Web and computer technology in general. Some of them have a lot of experience in the business world; for others, this is their first exposure to all of the issues involved in running a business.

In this case, it might be appropriate to create two personas. We'll call the first one Janet. She's 42 years old, she's married, and she has two kids. She's spent the last couple of years as a vice president at a large accounting firm. She's become frustrated with working for other people, and now she wants to build a company of her own.

The second persona is Frank. He's 37 years old and married with one child. Woodworking has been a weekend hobby of Frank's for many years. Some friends of his were impressed by some furniture he made, so he's been thinking he could go into business for himself selling his work. He's not sure if he'll have to quit his job as a school bus driver in order to launch his new business.

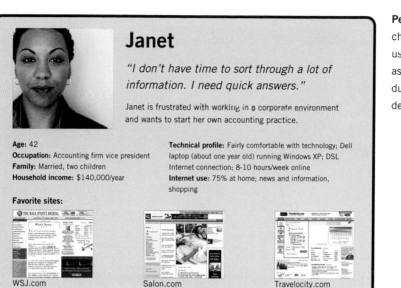

Janet

"I don't have time to sort through a lot of information. I need quick answers."

Janet is frustrated with working in a corporate environment and wants to start her own accounting practice.

Age: 42
Occupation: Accounting firm vice president
Family: Married, two children
Household income: $140,000/year

Technical profile: Fairly comfortable with technology; Dell laptop (about one year old) running Windows XP; DSL Internet connection; 8-10 hours/week online
Internet use: 75% at home; news and information, shopping

Favorite sites:

WSJ.com   Salon.com   Travelocity.com

Personas are fictional characters drawn from user research who serve as example cases during user experience development.

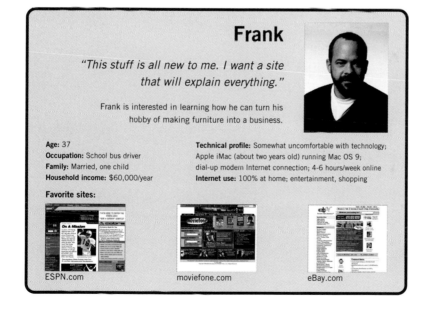

Frank

"This stuff is all new to me. I want a site that will explain everything."

Frank is interested in learning how he can turn his hobby of making furniture into a business.

Age: 37
Occupation: School bus driver
Family: Married, one child
Household income: $60,000/year

Technical profile: Somewhat uncomfortable with technology; Apple iMac (about two years old) running Mac OS 9; dial-up modem Internet connection; 4-6 hours/week online
Internet use: 100% at home; entertainment, shopping

Favorite sites:

ESPN.com   moviefone.com   eBay.com

Where did all this information come from? Well, for the most part, we made it up. We want our personas to be consistent with what we know about the users from our research, but the specific details of our personas are fictional inventions, used to breathe life into these characters who will stand in for our real live users.

Janet and Frank represent the range of user needs we'll have to keep in mind as we're making decisions about the user experience of our site. To help us remember them and their needs, we'll grab a couple of stock photos to give Janet and Frank a little more identity, and combine those photos with the information about them we've put together. These profiles can be printed out and posted around the office so that when we have decisions to make we can ask ourselves, "Would that work for Janet? How would Frank react to it?" The personas help us keep our users in mind every step of the way.

Team Roles and Process

Strategic issues affect everyone involved in the user experience development process. But despite this fact (or perhaps because of it), responsibility for formulating these objectives often falls through the cracks. Consulting firms will sometimes employ **strategists** on client projects to manage these issues—but because such rarefied expertise tends to be expensive, and because strategists aren't directly responsible for building any piece of the site itself, this line item is often one of the first to be cut from a project budget.

Strategists will talk to many people throughout the organization to get as many perspectives as possible on the questions of site objectives and user needs. **Stakeholders** are senior decision-makers who are responsible for parts of the organization that will be affected by the site strategy. For example, in the case of a site designed to provide customers with access to product support information, stakeholders might include representatives from marketing communications and customer service as well as product managers. It depends on the formal decision-making structure (and the informal political realities) of the organization.

One group often neglected in formulating a strategy are the rank and file—the people responsible for keeping the organization running on a day-to-day basis. But these people often have a better sense of what works and what doesn't than their managers do. They can inform the strategy in ways senior decision-makers can't—especially when it comes to user needs. No one knows what customers are having trouble with better than the people who talk to those customers every day. I am often surprised at how infrequently customer feedback finds its way to the product development teams who need it.

Site objectives and user needs are often defined in a formal **strategy document** or *vision document*. User needs are sometimes documented in a separate user research report (though there are certain advantages to having all your information in one place). This document isn't just a list of objectives—it provides an analysis of the relationship among the various objectives and of how those objectives fit into the larger context of the organization. The objectives and their analysis are often supported by direct quotes from stakeholders, rank-and-file employees, and users themselves. These quotes vividly illustrate the strategic issues involved in the project.

Bigger is not necessarily better when it comes to documenting your strategy. You don't have to include every data point and every supporting quote to get your point across. Keep it concise and to the point. Remember that many people who will be exposed to the document won't have the time or interest to wade through hundreds of pages of supporting material, and it's far more important that they understand the strategy than that they be impressed by the volume of verbiage you've produced. An effective strategy document not only serves as a touchstone for the user experience development team; it can also be used to build support for the project in other parts of the organization.

The worst thing you can do with your strategy document is limit your team's access to it. The document wasn't created to be filed away somewhere or shared only with a handful of senior staff members—if the effort that went into it is going to pay off, the document has to be used actively during the project. All participants—designers, programmers, information architects, project managers—need the strategy document to make informed decisions about their work. Strategy documents often contain sensitive material, but keeping them from the team responsible for realizing that strategy only undermines their ability to do so.

Strategy should be the beginning of your user experience development process, but that doesn't mean your strategy must be fixed in stone before the project can move forward. Although trying to hit a moving target can be a tremendous waste of time and resources (not to mention a huge source of internal frustration), strategies can and should evolve and be refined. When revised and refined systematically, strategy work can be a continuing source of inspiration throughout the process.

Further Reading

Cooper, Alan. *The Inmates Are Running the Asylum: Why High-Tech Products Drive Us Crazy and How to Restore the Sanity.* Sams, 1999.

Krug, Steve. *Don't Make Me Think: A Common Sense Approach to Web Usability.* New Riders, 2000.

Spool, Jared M., et al. *Web Site Usability: A Designer's Guide.* Morgan Kaufmann, 1998.

Web resources: **www.jjg.net/elements/resources/**.

chapter 4

The Scope Plane

Functional Specifications and Content Requirements

With a clear sense of what we want and what our

users want, we can figure out how to satisfy all

those strategic objectives. Strategy becomes scope

when you translate user needs and site objectives

into specific requirements for what content and

functionality the Web site will offer to users.

Surface

Skeleton

Structure

Scope

Strategy

Defining the Scope

We do some things because there's value in the process, like jogging or practicing scales on the piano. We do other things because there's value in the product, like making a cheesecake or fixing a car. Defining the scope of your project is both: a valuable process that results in a valuable product.

The *process* is valuable because it forces you to address potential conflicts and rough spots in the product while the whole thing is still hypothetical. We can identify what we can tackle now and what will have to wait until later.

The *product* is valuable because it gives the entire team a reference point for all the work to be done throughout the project and a common language for talking about that work. Defining your requirements drives ambiguity out of the development process.

I once worked on a Web application that seemed to be in a state of perpetual beta: almost, but not quite ready to roll out to actual users. A lot of things were wrong with our approach—the technology was shaky, we didn't seem to know anything about our users, and I was the only person in the whole company who had any experience with developing for the Web at all.

But none of this explains why we couldn't get the product to launch. The big stumbling block was an unwillingness to document requirements. After all, it was a lot of hassle to write everything down when we all worked in the same office anyway, and besides, the product manager needed to focus his energy on coming up with new features.

The result was a product that was an ever-changing mishmash of features in various stages of completeness. Every new article somebody read or every new thought that came along while somebody was playing with the product inspired another feature for consideration. There was a constant flow of work going on, but there was no schedule, there were no milestones, and there was no end in sight. Because no one knew the scope of the project, how could anyone know when we were finished?

There are two main reasons to go to the trouble of documenting requirements.

Reason #1: So You Know What You're Building

This seems kind of obvious, but it came as a surprise to the team building that Web application. If you write down a description of exactly what you're setting out to build, everyone will know what the project's goals are and when they've been reached. The final product stops being an amorphous picture in the product manager's head, and it becomes something concrete that everyone at every level of the organization, from top executives to entry-level engineers, can work with.

In the absence of documented requirements, your project will probably turn out like a schoolyard game of "Telephone"—each person on the team gets an impression of the product via word of mouth, and everyone's description ends up slightly different. Or even worse, everyone assumes someone else is managing some crucial aspect of the project, but in fact no one is.

Having a defined set of requirements allows you to parcel out responsibility for the work more efficiently. Seeing the entire scope mapped out enables you to see connections between individual requirements that might not otherwise be apparent. The support documentation and the product spec sheets may have seemed like separate content features in early discussions, but defining them as requirements might make it apparent that there's a lot of overlap and that the same group should be responsible for both.

Reason #2: So You Know What You're Not Building

Lots of features sound like good ideas, but they don't necessarily align with the strategic objectives of the project. Additionally, all sorts of possibilities for features emerge after the project is well underway. Having documented requirements provides you with a framework for evaluating those ideas as they come along.

Requirements that can't be met in the current schedule can form the basis for the next milestone in your development cycle.

Knowing what you're not building also means knowing what you're not building *right now*. The real value in collecting all those great ideas comes from finding appropriate ways to fit them into your long-term plans. By establishing concrete sets of development requirements and stockpiling any requests that don't fit those requirements as possibilities for future releases, you can manage the entire process in a more deliberate and conscious way.

If you don't consciously manage your requirements, you'll get caught in the dreaded "scope creep." The image this always brings to mind for me is the snowball that rolls forward only an inch—and then another—picking up a little extra snow with each turn until it is careening down the hill, getting bigger and harder to stop all the way down. Likewise, each additional requirement may not seem like that much extra work. But put them all together, and you've got a project rolling away out of control, blowing past deadlines and budget estimates on its way toward an inevitable final crash.

Functionality and Content

On the scope plane, we turn from the abstract question of "Why are we making this site?" that we dealt with in the strategy plane and build upon it with a new question: "What are we going to make?"

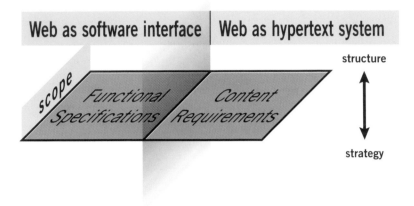

The split between the Web as a software interface and the Web as a hypertext system starts coming into play on the scope plane. On the software side, we're concerned with functionality—what would be considered the "feature set" of the software product. On the hypertext side, we're dealing with content, the traditional domain of editorial and marketing communications groups.

Content and functionality seem just about as different as two things could be, but when it comes to defining scope, they can be addressed in very similar ways. Throughout this chapter, I'll use the term "feature" to refer to both software functions and content offerings.

In software development, the scope is defined in the functional requirements or **functional specifications** documents. Some organizations use these terms to mean two different documents: requirements at the beginning of the project to describe what the system should do, and specifications at the end to describe what it actually does do. In other cases, the specifications are developed soon after the requirements, filling in details of implementation. But most of the time, these terms are interchangeable—in fact, some people use the term "functional requirements specification" just to make sure they've covered all the bases. I'll use "functional specifications" to refer to the document itself, and "requirements" to refer to its contents.

The language of this chapter is mostly the language of software development. But the concepts here apply equally to content. Content development often does not involve as formal a requirements-gathering process as software does, but the underlying principles are the same. A content developer will sit down and talk with people or pore over source material, whether that be a database or a drawer full of news clippings, in order to determine what information needs to be included in the content she's developing. This less formal process for gathering **content requirements** is actually not all that different from the technologist brainstorming features with stakeholders and reviewing existing documentation. The purposes and approaches are the same.

Content requirements often have functional implications. These days, content is usually handled by a **content management system (CMS)**. These systems come in all shapes and sizes, from very large and complex systems that dynamically generate pages from a dozen different data sources to lightweight tools optimized for managing one specific type of content feature in the most efficient way. You might decide to purchase a proprietary content management system, use one of the many open-source alternatives, or even build one from scratch. In any case, it will take some tinkering to tailor the system to your organization and your content.

A **content management system** can automate the workflow required to produce and deliver content to users.

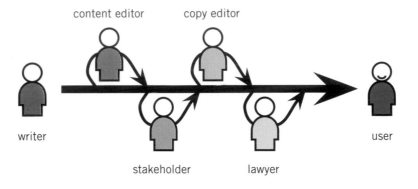

The functionality you will need in your content management system will depend on the nature of the content you'll be managing. Will you be maintaining content in multiple languages or data formats? The CMS will need to be able to handle all those kinds of content elements. Does every press release need to be approved by six executive vice presidents and a lawyer? The CMS will need to support that kind of approval process in its workflow. Will content elements be dynamically recombined according to the preferences of each user? The CMS will need to be able to accomplish that level of complex delivery.

Similarly, functional requirements have content implications. Will there be instructions on the preferences configuration screen? How about error messages? Somebody has to write those. Every time I see an error message on a Web site like "Null input field exception," I know some engineer's placeholder message made it into the final product because nobody made that error message a content requirement. Countless allegedly technical projects could have been improved immeasurably if the developers had simply taken the time to have someone look at the application with an eye toward content.

Gathering Requirements

Some requirements apply to the site as a whole. Branding requirements are one common example of this; certain technical requirements, such as supported browsers and operating systems, are another.

Other requirements apply only to a specific feature. Most of the time when people refer to a requirement, they are thinking of a short description of a single feature the product is required to have.

The most productive source for requirements will always be your users themselves. The best way to find out what people want is simply *to ask them*. The user research techniques outlined in Chapter 3 can all be used to help you get a better understanding of the kinds of features users want to see on your site.

Whether you are gathering requirements from stakeholders inside your organization or getting them directly from users, the requirements that come out of the process will fall into three general categories. First, and most obvious, are the things people say they want. Some of these are very clearly good ideas and will find their way into the final product.

Sometimes the things people say they want are not really good ideas, but they represent a path to the next type of requirement: things they *actually* want. It's not uncommon for anyone, when they encounter some difficulty with a process or a product, to imagine a solution that will alleviate that difficulty. Sometimes that solution is unworkable, or it addresses a symptom rather than the underlying disease. By exploring these suggestions, you can sometimes arrive at completely different requirements that solve the real problem.

The third type of requirement to come out of this process is the feature people don't know they want. When you get people talking about new requirements and strategic objectives, sometimes they'll hit upon great ideas that simply hadn't occurred to anyone during the ongoing maintenance of the site. These often come out of brainstorming exercises, when participants have had a chance to talk through and explore the possibilities for the project.

Ironically, sometimes the people least able to imagine new directions for a site are those most deeply involved in creating and working with it. For this reason, group brainstorming sessions that bring together people from diverse parts of the organization or represent diverse user groups can be very effective tools in opening the minds of participants to possibilities they wouldn't have considered before.

Getting an engineer, a customer service agent, and a marketing person in a room together to talk about the same Web site can be enlightening for everyone. Hearing perspectives on the site other than those they are familiar with—and having the opportunity to respond to them—encourages people to think in broader terms about both the problems involved in developing the site and the possible solutions.

Generating requirements is often a matter of finding ways to remove impediments. Assume that you have a user who has already decided to make a purchase—they just haven't decided if your product is the one they will buy. What can your site do to make this process—first selecting your product, and then buying your product—easier for them?

In Chapter 3, we looked at the technique of creating fictional characters called personas to help us better understand user needs. In determining requirements, we can use those personas again by putting our fictional characters into little stories called **scenarios**. A scenario is a short, simple narrative describing how a persona might go about trying to fulfill one of those user needs. By imagining the process our users might go through, we can come up with potential requirements that will meet their needs.

We can also look to our competitors for inspiration. Anyone else in the same business is almost certainly trying to meet the same user needs and is probably trying to accomplish similar site objectives as well. Has a competitor found a particularly effective feature for reaching one of these strategic goals? How have they addressed the tradeoffs and compromises we face?

Even sites that aren't direct competitors can serve as fertile sources for possible requirements. Most corporate sites, for example, offer information about employment opportunities. By looking at how companies outside our own industry have handled this type of content, we may find an approach that gives us an advantage over our direct competition.

The level of detail in your requirements will often depend on the specific scope of the project. If the goal of the project is to implement one very complex subsystem, a very high level of detail might be needed, even though the scope of the project relative to the larger site might be quite small. Conversely, a very large-scale content project might involve such a homogeneous base of content that the content requirements can only be very general.

Functional Specifications

Functional specifications have something of a bad reputation in certain quarters. Programmers often hate specs because they tend to be terribly dull, and the time spent reading them is time taken away from producing code. As a result, specs go unread, which in turn reinforces the impression that producing them is a waste of time.

One complaint about functional specifications is that they don't reflect the actual product. Things change during implementation. Everybody understands this—it's the nature of working with technology. Sometimes something you thought would work didn't, or more likely didn't quite work the way you thought it would. This, however, is not a reason to abandon writing specs as a lost cause. Instead, it highlights the importance of keeping specs and keeping them up-to-date. When things change during implementation, the answer is not to throw up your hands and declare the futility of writing specs. The answer is to be vigilant about keeping the spec in sync with development.

But no matter how large or complex the project may be, a few general rules apply to writing any kind of requirements.

Be positive. Instead of describing a bad thing the system shouldn't do, describe what it will do to prevent that bad thing. For example, instead of this:

> *The system will not allow the user to purchase a kite without kite string.*

This would be better:

> *The system will direct the user to the kite string page if the user tries to buy a kite without string.*

Be specific. Leaving as little as possible open to interpretation is the only way we can determine whether a requirement has been fulfilled.

Compare these examples:

1. *The site will be accessible to disabled people.*
2. *The site will comply with Section 508 of the Rehabilitation Act.*

The first example seems to identify a clear requirement, but it does not take much investigation to start poking holes in it. What counts as "accessible?" If the site provides text descriptions of all images, is that sufficient? And who counts as a disabled person? If the site doesn't rely on audio, it must therefore be accessible to the deaf—is that sufficient?

Fortunately, somebody else has worked out all these definitions and distinctions for us: the U.S. Congress. The second example refers us to the specific legal document that defines our goal in specific detail. By removing the possibility of differing interpretations, the second requirement neatly skirts the kinds of arguments likely to crop up during or after implementation.

Avoid subjective language. This is really just another way of being specific and removing ambiguity—and therefore the possibility for misinterpretation—from the requirements.

Here's a highly subjective requirement:

The site will have a hip, flashy style.

Requirements must be falsifiable—that is, it must be possible to demonstrate when a requirement has not been met. It's difficult to demonstrate whether subjective qualities like "hip" and "flashy" have been fulfilled. My idea of hipness probably doesn't match yours, and most likely the CEO has another idea entirely.

This doesn't mean you can't require that your site be hip. You just have to find ways to specify which criteria will be applied:

The site will meet the hipness expectations of Wayne, the mail clerk.

Wayne normally wouldn't have any say about the project, but our project sponsor clearly respects his sense of hipness. Hopefully it's the same sense our users have. But the requirement is still rather arbitrary because we're relying on Wayne's sense of style instead of criteria that can be more objectively defined. So perhaps this requirement would be best of all:

The look of the site will conform to the company branding guidelines document.

The whole concept of hipness has now disappeared entirely from the requirement. Instead, we have a clear, unambiguous reference to established guidelines. To make sure the branding guidelines are sufficiently hip, the VP of marketing may consult Wayne the mail clerk, or she may consult her teenage daughter, or she may even consult some user research findings. It's up to her. But now we can say definitively whether the requirement has been met.

We can also eliminate subjectivity by defining some requirements in quantitative terms. Just as success metrics make strategic goals quantifiable, defining a requirement in quantitative terms can help us clearly identify whether we've met the requirement. For example, instead of requiring that the system have "a high level of performance," we can require that the system be designed to support at least 1,000 simultaneous users. If the final product only has a three-digit user number field, we can tell the requirement hasn't been met.

Content Requirements

Much of the time, when we talk about content, we're referring to text. But we should remember that images, audio, and video are also types of content. These different content types can also work together to fulfill a single requirement. For example, a content feature covering a sporting event might have an article accompanied by photographs and video clips. Identifying all the different content types associated with a given feature can help you determine what resources will be needed to produce the content (or whether it can be produced at all).

Don't get confused between the *format* of a piece of content and its *purpose*. When discussing content requirements with stakeholders, one of the first things I usually hear is something like, "We should have FAQs on the site." But the term "FAQ" really only refers to a content format: a simple series of questions and answers. The real value a FAQ provides to users is that it provides ready access to commonly needed information. Other content requirements can fulfill that same purpose; but when the focus is on the format, the purpose itself can be forgotten. More often than not, FAQs neglect the "frequently" part of the equation, offering instead answers to whatever questions the content provider could think of to satisfy the FAQ requirement.

The expected size of each of your content features has a huge influence on the user experience decisions you will have to make. Your content requirements should provide rough estimates of the size of each feature: word count for text features, pixel dimensions for images, and file sizes for downloadable, stand-alone content elements like PDF documents, or for features like audio or video. These size estimates don't have to be precise—approximations will suffice. We only have to collect the essential information we need to design an appropriate site around that content. Designing a site to provide access to small thumbnail images is different from designing a site to provide access to full-screen photographs; knowing in advance the size of the content elements we have to accommodate allows us to make smart, informed decisions along the way.

It's important to identify who will be responsible for each content element as early as possible. Once it has been validated against our strategic objectives, any content feature inevitably sounds like a really good idea—as long as someone else is responsible for creating and maintaining it. If we get too deep into the development process without identifying who will be responsible for every required content feature, we're likely to end up with gaping holes in our site because those features everybody loved when they were still hypothetical turned out to be too much work for anyone to actually take on.

And that's what people often forget when developing requirements: content is hard work. You might be able to hire on contract resources (or, more likely, stick someone down in marketing with the job) to create the content in time for the initial launch, but who will keep it up to date? Content—well, effective content, anyway—requires constant maintenance. Approaching content as if you can post it and forget it leads to a site that, over time, does an increasingly poor job of meeting user needs.

This is why, for every content feature, you should identify how frequently it will be updated. The frequency of updates should be derived from your strategic goals for the site: Based on your site objectives, how often do you want users to come back? Based on the needs of your users, how often do they expect updated information? However, keep in mind that the ideal frequency of updates for your users ("I want to know everything instantly, 24 hours a day!") may not be practical for your organization. You'll have to arrive at a frequency that represents a reasonable compromise between the expectations of your users and your available resources.

If your site has to serve multiple audiences, it can be useful to identify which audience a content feature is intended for. Particularly in cases where audiences have divergent needs, knowing which audience a piece of content is intended for can help us make better decisions about how to present that content. Information intended for children requires a different approach from information intended for their parents; information for both of them needs yet a third treatment.

For projects that involve working with a lot of existing content (rather than content that has to be created from scratch), much of this information about content is recorded in a **content inventory**. Taking an inventory of all the content on your existing site may seem like a tedious process—and it usually is. But having the inventory (which usually takes the form of a simple, albeit very large, spreadsheet) is important for the same reason that having concrete requirements is important: so everyone on the team knows exactly what they have to work with in creating the user experience.

Prioritizing Requirements

Collecting ideas for possible requirements is not hard. Almost everyone who regularly comes in contact with a product—whether they are inside the organization or outside—will have at least one idea for a feature that could be added. The tricky part is sorting out what features should be included in the scope for your project.

It's actually fairly rare that you see a simple one-to-one correlation between your strategic objectives and your requirements. Sometimes one requirement can be applied toward multiple strategic objectives. Similarly, one objective will often be associated with several different requirements.

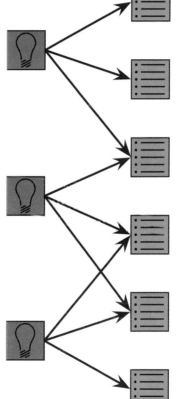

Sometimes a strategic objective will result in multiple requirements (left). In other cases, one requirement can serve multiple strategic objectives (right).

Because the scope is built upon the strategy, we'll need to evaluate possible requirements based on whether they fulfill our strategic goals (both site objectives and user needs). In addition to those two considerations, defining the scope adds a third: How feasible will it be to actually make this stuff?

Some features can't be implemented because they're technically impossible—for example, there's just no way to allow users to smell products over the Web yet, no matter how badly they might want that ability. Other features (particularly in the case of content) aren't feasible because they would just demand more resources—whether human or financial—than we have at our disposal. In other cases, it's just a matter of time: the feature would take three months to implement, but we have an executive requirement to launch in two.

In the case of time constraints, you can push features out to a later release or project milestone. For resource constraints, technological or organizational changes can sometimes—but, importantly, not always—reduce the resource burden, enabling a feature to be implemented. (However, impossible things will remain impossible. Sorry.)

Few features exist in a vacuum. Even content features on a Web site rely upon the features around them to support and inform the user on how best to use the content provided. This inevitably leads to conflicts between features. Some features will require tradeoffs with others in order to produce a coherent, consistent whole. For example, some users may want a one-step order submission process—but the tangle of legacy databases the site needs to work with can't accommodate all the data at once. Is it preferable to go with a multiple-step process, or should you rework the database system? It depends on your strategic objectives.

Keep an eye out for feature suggestions that indicate possible shifts in strategy that weren't apparent during the development of the vision document. Any feature suggestion not in line with the project strategy is, by definition, out of scope. But if a suggested feature that falls outside the scope doesn't fit any of the types of constraints above and still sounds like a good idea, you may need to re-examine some of your strategic objectives. If you find yourself revisiting strategy, however, you've probably jumped into gathering requirements too soon.

If your strategy or vision document identifies a clear hierarchy of priorities among your strategic objectives, these priorities should be the primary factors in determining the relative priority of suggested features. Sometimes, however, the relative importance of two different strategic objectives isn't clear. In these cases, whether features end up in the project scope all too often comes down to corporate politics.

When stakeholders talk about strategy, they usually start out with feature ideas, and then have to be coaxed back to the underlying strategic factors. Because stakeholders often have trouble separating features from strategy, certain features will often have champions during the requirements process. Thus the requirements gathering process becomes a matter of negotiation between motivated stakeholders.

Managing this negotiation process can be difficult. The best approach to resolving a conflict between stakeholders is to appeal to the defined strategy. Focus on strategic goals, not proposed means of accomplishing them. If you can assure a stakeholder with her heart set on a particular feature that the strategic goal the feature is intended to fulfill can be addressed in some other way, she won't feel the needs of her constituents are being neglected. Admittedly, this is often easier said than done. Demonstrating empathy with the needs of stakeholders is essential to resolving feature conflicts. Who says tech workers don't need people skills?

Further Reading

Wiegers, Karl E. *Software Requirements*. Microsoft Press, 1999.

Robertson, Suzanne and James Robertson. *Mastering the Requirements Process*. Addison Wesley, 1999.

Web resources: **www.jjg.net/elements/resources/**.

The Structure Plane

Interaction Design and Information Architecture

After the requirements have been collected and

prioritized, we have a clear picture of what will be

included in the final product. The requirements,

however, don't describe how the pieces fit together

to form a cohesive whole. This is the next level up

from scope: developing a conceptual structure for

the site.

Defining the Structure

The realm of structure is the third of the five planes, and appropriately it is the point at which our concerns shift from the more abstract issues of strategy and scope to the concrete factors that will determine what users finally experience. But the line between abstract and concrete can sometimes become blurry—although much of what we decide here will have a noticeable, tangible influence on the final site, the decisions themselves still involve largely conceptual matters.

In traditional software development, the discipline involved in creating a structured experience for the user is known as **interaction design**. It used to be lumped under the heading of "interface design," but in recent years (due partly to the advent of Web applications and partly to the dedicated evangelism of its practitioners) interaction design has come into its own as a unique discipline.

In content development, structuring the user experience is a question of **information architecture**. This field draws on a number of disciplines that historically have been concerned with the organization, grouping, ordering, and presentation of content: library science, journalism, and technical communication, among others.

Interaction design and information architecture share an emphasis on defining patterns and sequences in which options will be presented to users. Interaction design concerns the options involved in performing and completing tasks. Information architecture deals with the options involved in conveying information to a user.

Interaction design and information architecture sound like esoteric, highly technical areas, but these disciplines aren't really about technology at all. They're about *understanding people, the way they work, and the way they think.* By building this understanding into the structure of our product, we help ensure a successful experience for those who have to use it.

Interaction Design

Interaction design is concerned with describing possible user behavior and defining how the system will accommodate and respond to that behavior. Anytime a person uses a computer, a sort of dance goes on between the user and the machine. The user moves around, and the system responds. The user moves in response to the system, and so the dance goes on. But the typical way that software has been designed doesn't really acknowledge this dance. The thinking seems to have been that if every application danced a little bit differently anyway, it wasn't unreasonable to expect the user to adapt. The system could just do its thing, and if some toes got stepped on, well, that was part of the learning process. But every dancer will tell you that for the dance to really work, each participant must anticipate the moves of the other.

Programmers have traditionally focused on and cared most about two aspects of software: what it does and how it does it. There's a good reason for this—it is precisely their passion for these details that makes programmers good at what they do. But this focus meant that programmers could go ahead and build the system in the way that was most technically efficient without regard to what worked best for users. Especially back when computing power was a limited resource, the best approach was the one that got the job done within those system limitations.

The approach that works best for the computer is almost never the approach that works best for the person who has to use it. Thus, computer software acquired the reputation that has haunted it for most of its existence: Software is complicated, confusing, and hard to use. Only 10 years ago, "computer literacy"—teaching people about the inner workings of computers—was widely considered to be the only way to make users and software get along.

It took a long time, but as computers became more powerful and we learned more about how people used them, eventually we started catching on to the idea that, instead of designing software to work in the fashion that works best for the machine, we could design software to work in the fashion that works best for the people who use it, thereby skipping this whole business of sending file clerks to programming classes to improve their computer literacy. The new discipline that arose to help software developers do this is called interaction design.

Conceptual Models

Users' impressions of how the interactive components we create will behave are known as **conceptual models**. For example, is it a content element, a place the user visits, or an object the user acquires? Different sites take different approaches. Knowing your conceptual model allows you to make consistent design decisions. It doesn't matter whether the content element is a place or an object; what matters is that the site behaves consistently, instead of treating the element as a place sometimes and an object at other times.

For example, the conceptual model for the "shopping cart" component of a typical e-commerce site is that of a container. This metaphorical concept influences both the design of the component and the language we use in the interface. A container holds objects; as a result, we "put things into" and "take things out of" the "cart," and the system must provide functions to accomplish these tasks.

Suppose the conceptual model for the component were a different real-world analogue, such as a catalog order form. The system might provide an "edit" function that would replace both the "add" and "remove" functions of the traditional cart, and instead of using a "checkout" metaphor to complete the process, users might "send" their orders in.

Both the retail store model and the catalog model seem perfectly suitable for allowing users to place orders over the Web. Which to choose? The retail store model is so widely used on the Web that it's taken on the status of a **convention**. If your users do a lot of shopping on other Web sites, you'll probably want to stick to that convention. Using conceptual models people are familiar with makes it easier for them to adapt to an unfamiliar site. Of course, there's nothing wrong with breaking from convention either—as long as you have a good reason for doing so and have an alternate conceptual model that will meet your users' needs.

A conceptual model can refer to just one component of a system or to the system as a whole. When the news and commentary site Slate launched, its conceptual model was a real-world magazine: The site had a front and a back, and every page had both a page number and interface elements allowing the user to "turn the page." As it turns out, the magazine conceptual model doesn't translate very effectively to the Web, and Slate eventually dropped the magazine concept.

We don't have to communicate our conceptual models to our users explicitly—in fact, sometimes this only confuses users instead of helping them. It's more important that conceptual models are used consistently throughout the development of the interaction design. Understanding the models users themselves bring to the site (Does it work like a retail store? Does it work like a catalog?) helps us choose conceptual models that will work most effectively. Ideally, the users won't have to be told what conceptual model we're following; they'll pick up on it intuitively as they use the site because the behavior of the site will match their expectations.

Basing our conceptual models on metaphors involving real-world analogues to system functions can be valuable, but it's important not to take our metaphors too literally. The home page of the site for Southwest Airlines used to consist solely of a picture of a customer service desk, with a stack of brochures to one side, a telephone to the other side, and so on. For years, the site was held up as an example of a conceptual model gone too far—placing a reservation may be analogous to making a phone call, but that doesn't mean the reservation system should actually be represented by a telephone. Southwest must have gotten tired of being used as a bad example; today their site is light on metaphor and considerably more functional.

The old Southwest Airlines site is a classic example of conceptual models being tied too closely to real-world counterparts.

The redesigned Southwest Airlines site makes content and functionality more directly apparent.

Error Handling

A huge part of any interaction design project involves dealing with "user error"—what does the system do when people make mistakes, and what can the system do to prevent those mistakes from happening in the first place?

The first and best defense against errors is to design the system so that errors are simply impossible. A good example of this type of defense can be seen in any car with an automatic transmission. Starting the car while the transmission is engaged can damage the sensitive and complex transmission mechanism; moreover, the car doesn't actually start, but instead lurches forward abruptly. Bad for the car, bad for the driver, and possibly bad for an innocent bystander who happens to be in the path of the lurching car.

To prevent this, any car with an automatic transmission is designed so the starter won't engage unless the transmission is disengaged. Because it's impossible to start the car with the transmission engaged, the error never happens. Unfortunately, it's not quite so easy to make most user errors impossible in this way.

The next best thing to making errors impossible is to make them merely difficult. But even with such measures in place, some errors are bound to happen. At this point, the system should do what it can to help the user figure out the error and fix it. In some cases, the system can even fix the error on the user's behalf. But be careful—some of the most irritating behavior of software products results from well-intentioned efforts to correct user errors. (If you've ever used Microsoft Word, you know exactly what I'm talking about. Word offers numerous features intended to correct common errors; invariably, I find myself switching them off so I can get some work done and stop correcting the corrections.)

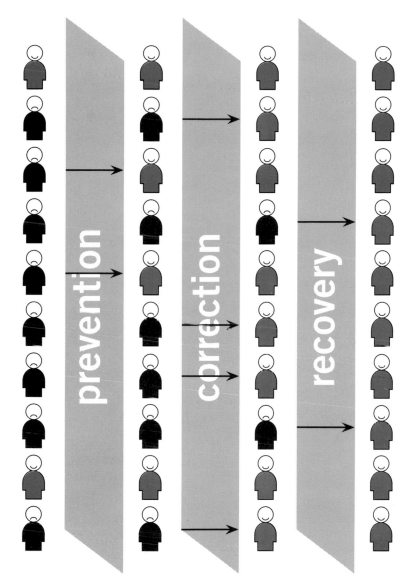

Each layer of error handling in your interaction design ensures that a higher percentage of users will have positive experiences.

Helpful error messages and well-designed interfaces can help users catch many kinds of errors after they've happened. But some user actions may not appear to be errors until it's too late even for the system to catch them. In these cases, the system should provide a way for users to recover from the error. The best-known example of this is the famous "undo" function, but error recovery can take many different forms. For errors that can't be recovered from, providing plenty of warning is the only means of prevention the system can provide. Of course, this warning is only effective when users actually notice it, which is why a succession of "Are you sure?" dialog boxes often annoys more users than it helps.

Information Architecture

Information architecture is concerned with creating organizational and navigational schemes that allow users to move through site content efficiently and effectively. Information architecture is closely related to the concept of information retrieval: the design of systems that enable users to find information easily. But Web site architectures are often called on to do more than just help people find things; in many cases, they have to educate, inform, or persuade users.

Most commonly, information architecture problems require creating categorization schemes that will correspond to our own objectives for the site, the user needs we intend to meet, and the content that will be incorporated in the site. We can tackle creating such a categorization scheme in two ways: from the top down, or from the bottom up.

Top-down architectural
approach.

A **top-down approach** to information architecture involves creating the architecture directly from an understanding of site objectives
and user needs. Starting with the broadest categories of possible content and functionality needed to accomplish these strategic goals, we
then break the categories down into logical subsections. This hierarchy of categories and sub-categories serves as the empty shell into
which the content and functionality will be slotted.

A **bottom-up approach** to information architecture also derives
categories and sub-categories, but it does so based on an analysis of
the content and functional requirements. Starting with the source
material that exists (or that will exist by the time the site launches),
we group items together into low-level categories and then group
those into higher-level categories, building toward a structure that
reflects our site objectives and user needs.

Bottom-up architectural
approach.

Neither approach is better than the other. Approaching the architecture from the top down can sometimes cause important details about the content itself to be overlooked. On the other hand, a bottom-up approach can sometimes result in an architecture so precisely tuned and fitted to the existing content that it isn't flexible enough to accommodate changes or additions. Striking a balance between top-down and bottom-up thinking is the only way to make sure the final result can avoid these pitfalls.

Web sites are living entities. They require constant care and feeding. Inevitably, they grow and change over time. In most cases, a few new requirements acquired along the way shouldn't require rethinking the overall structure of the site. One trait of an effective structure is its ability to accommodate growth and adapt to change. But the accumulation of new content will eventually require a re-examination of the organizing principles employed on the site. For example, the architecture that enabled users to page through press releases day by day might have been fine when you had only a few months' worth, but organizing them by topic might be more practical after a few years.

It's not necessary to adhere to a particular number of categories at any level or in any section of the architecture. The categories just have to be the right ones for your users and their needs. Some people favor counting the number of steps it takes to complete a task or the number of clicks it takes for a user to reach a particular destination as a way to evaluate the quality of a site structure. The most important sign of quality, however, is not how many steps the process took, but whether each step made sense to the user and whether it followed naturally from the previous step. Users will invariably favor a clearly defined seven-step process over a confusingly compressed three-step alternative.

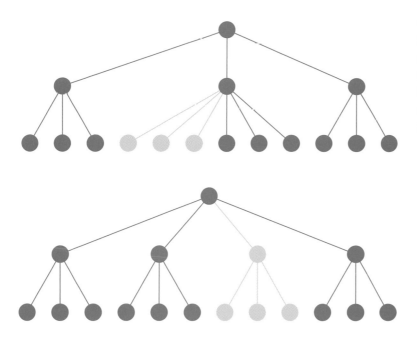

An adaptable architecture can accommodate the addition of new content within a section (top) as well as entire new sections (bottom).

The entire user experience, including the structure of the site, is built on an understanding of your objectives and the needs of your users. If what you want to accomplish with the site is redefined or the needs you intend the site to meet change, be prepared to rework the structure of your site accordingly. The need for such structural changes rarely announces itself in advance, though; often, by the time you can tell that you need to rework the architecture, your users are already suffering.

Architectural Approaches

The basic unit of information structures is the **node**. A node can correspond to any piece or group of information—it can be as small as a single number (like the price of a product) or as large as an entire library. By dealing with nodes rather than with pages, documents, or components, we can apply a common language and a common set of structural concepts to a diverse range of problems.

The abstraction of nodes also allows us to explicitly set the level of detail we will be concerned with. Most Web site architecture projects are only concerned with the arrangement of pages on the site; by identifying the page as our base-level node, we make it explicit that we won't be dealing with anything smaller. If the page itself is too small for the project at hand, we can have each node correspond to an entire section of the site.

These nodes can be arranged in many different ways, but these structures really fall into just a few general classes.

In a **hierarchical** structure—sometimes called a *tree* or *hub-and-spoke* structure—nodes have parent/child relationships with other related nodes. Child nodes represent narrower concepts within the broader category represented by the parent node. Not every node has children, but every node has a parent, leading all the way up to the parent node of the entire structure (or the "root" of the "tree," if you prefer). Because the concept of hierarchical relationships is well understood by users and because computers tend to work in hierarchies anyway, this type of structure is far and away the most common.

Hierarchical structure.

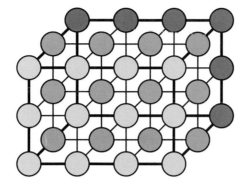

Matrix structure.

A **matrix** structure allows the user to move from node to node along two or more "dimensions." Matrix structures are often useful for enabling users with different needs to navigate through the same content, because each user need can be associated with one "axis" of the matrix. For example, if some of your users really want to browse products by color, but others need to browse by size, a matrix can accommodate both groups. A matrix of more than three dimensions can cause problems, however, if you expect users to rely on it as their primary navigational tool. The human brain simply isn't very well equipped to visualize movement in four or more dimensions.

Organic structures don't attempt to follow any consistent pattern. Nodes are connected together on a case-by-case basis, and the architecture has no strong concept of "sections." Organic structures are good for exploring a set of topics whose relationship is unclear or evolving. But organic structures don't provide users with a strong sense of where they are in the architecture. If you want to encourage a feeling of free-form exploration, such as on some entertainment or educational sites, an organic structure can be a good choice; however, it can present a challenge if your users need to reliably find their way back to the same piece of content again.

Organic structure.

Sequential structure.

Sequential structures are the ones you are most familiar with from offline media—in fact, you're experiencing one right now. The sequential flow of language is the most basic type of information architecture there is, and the facilities needed to process it are built right into our brains. Books, articles, audio, and video are all designed to be experienced in a sequential fashion. Sequential structures on the Web are used most often for smaller-scale structures such as individual articles or sections; large-scale sequential structures tend to be limited to applications in which the order of content presentation is essential to meeting user needs, such as in instructional material.

Organizing Principles

Nodes in an information structure are arranged according to **organizing principles**. At its most basic level, the organizing principle is the criterion by which we determine which nodes are grouped together and which are kept separate. Different organizing principles will be applied in different areas and at different levels of the site.

For example, in the case of a corporate information site, we might have categories near the top of our tree, such as "Consumer," "Business," and "Investor." At this level, the organizing principle is the audience for which the content is intended. Another site might have top-level categories like "North America," "Europe," and "Africa." Using geography as an organizing principle is one approach to meeting the needs of a global audience of users.

Generally, the organizing principles you employ at the highest levels of your site are closely tied to the site objectives and user needs. At lower levels in the architecture, issues specific to the content and functional requirements begin to have a greater influence on the organizing principles that should be used.

For example, a site with news-oriented content will often have chronology as its most prominent organizing principle. Timeliness is the single most important factor for users (who, after all, look to news sites for information on current events, not history) as well as for the creators of the site (who must emphasize the timeliness of their content in order to remain competitive).

At the next level in the architecture, other factors more closely tied to content come into play. For a sports news site, the content might be divided into categories such as "Baseball," "Tennis," and "Hockey"; a more general-interest site might have categories like "International News," "National News," and "Local News."

Any collection of information—whether it consists of two items, 200, or 2,000—has an inherent conceptual structure. In fact, it usually has more than one. That's part of the problem we have to solve. The challenge isn't creating a structure, but creating the *right* structure for our objectives and the needs of our users.

For example, suppose our site contained a repository of information about cars. One possible organizing principle would arrange the information according to the weight of the car in question. So the first thing the user would see would be information about the heaviest car in our database, then the second heaviest, and on down to the lightest.

For a consumer information site, this is probably the wrong way to organize the information. Most people, most of the time, aren't concerned with the weight of a car. Organizing the information according to make, model, or type of car would probably be more appropriate for this audience. On the other hand, if our users are professionals who deal on a daily basis with the business of shipping cars overseas, weight becomes a very important factor. For these people, qualities like fuel economy and engine type are considerably less important, if they matter at all.

These attributes, in the language of library science, are known as **facets**, and they can provide a simple, flexible set of organizing principles for almost any content. But as the preceding example shows, using the wrong facets can be worse than using no facets at all. One common response to this problem is to position every conceivable facet as an organizing principle and let the users pick the one that's important to them.

Unfortunately, unless you're dealing with very simple information consisting of only a few facets, this approach soon turns the architecture into an unwieldy mess. The users have so many options to sort through that no one can find anything. The burden shouldn't be on the user to sort through all the attributes and pick out what's important—the burden is on us. The strategy tells us what the users need, and the scope tells us what information will meet those needs. In creating the structure, we identify the specific aspects of that information that will be foremost in the users' minds. A successful user experience is one in which the user's expectations are anticipated in advance.

Language and Metadata

Even if the structure is a perfectly accurate representation of the way users think about your subject matter, they won't be able to find their way around the architecture if they can't understand your **nomenclature**: the descriptions, labels, and other terminology the site uses. For this reason, it's essential to use the language of your users and to do so in a consistent fashion. The tool we use to enforce that consistency is called a **controlled vocabulary**.

A controlled vocabulary is nothing more than a set of standard terms for use on the site. This is another area in which user research is essential. Talking to users and understanding how they communicate is the most effective way to develop a system of nomenclature that will feel natural to them. Creating a controlled vocabulary that reflects the language of your users (and adhering to it) is the best way to prevent your organization's internal jargon from creeping onto the site, where it will only confuse your users.

Controlled vocabularies also help create consistency across all your content. Whether the people responsible for producing the content sit right next to each other or in offices on separate continents, the controlled vocabulary provides a definitive resource to ensure that everyone is speaking the user's language.

A more sophisticated approach to controlling vocabulary is to create a **thesaurus**. Unlike a simple list of approved terms, a thesaurus will also document alternative terms that are commonly used but not approved for use on the site. With a thesaurus, you can map internal jargon, shorthand, slang terms, or acronyms to their approved counterparts. A thesaurus might also include other types of relationships among the terms, providing recommendations for broader, narrower, or related terms. Documenting these relationships can give you a more complete picture of the entire range of concepts found in your content, which in turn can suggest additional architectural approaches.

Having a controlled vocabulary or thesaurus can be especially helpful if you decide to build a system that includes **metadata**. The term
metadata means simply "information about information." It refers to
a structured approach to describing a given piece of content.

Suppose we were dealing with an article about how your latest
product is being used by volunteer fire departments. Some of the
metadata for that article might include:

- ▶ The name of the author
- ▶ The date the piece was posted
- ▶ The type of piece (for example, a case study or article)
- ▶ The name of the product
- ▶ The type of product
- ▶ The customer's industry (for example, volunteer fire
  department)
- ▶ Other relevant information (for example, municipal agencies
  or emergency services)

Having this information allows us to consider a range of possible
architectural approaches that would be difficult (if not downright
impossible) to implement without it. In short, the more detailed
information you have about your content, the more flexibility you
have in structuring it. If emergency services suddenly shows potential as a lucrative new market for the company to expand into,
having this metadata will allow us to rapidly create a new section to
meet the needs of these users with the content we already have.

But creating technical systems to collect and track all this metadata won't help us if the data itself isn't consistent. That's where controlled vocabularies come in. By using only one term for each unique concept in your content, you can rely on automation to help define the connections between your content elements. Your site could dynamically link together all the pages on a specific topic without anyone having to do anything more than use the same term consistently in their metadata.

In addition, good metadata can provide a faster and more reliable way for your users to find information on your site than a basic full-text search engine can provide. Search engines can be powerful, but in general they're very, very dumb—you give them a string of characters, and they pretty much go looking for exactly that string of characters. They don't understand what any of it means.

Connecting your search engine with a thesaurus and providing metadata for your content can help make the engine smarter. The search engine can use the thesaurus to map a search for a disallowed term to a preferred term; then it can check the metadata for that preferred term. Instead of getting no results at all, the user gets highly targeted, relevant results—and maybe even some recommendations for other related subjects that might be of interest.

Team Roles and Process

The documents needed to describe the structure of a site—from the specific details of nomenclature and metadata to the big picture of overall information architecture and interaction design—can vary substantially depending on the complexity of the project. For projects involving a lot of content in a hierarchical structure, simple text outlines can be an effective way to document the architecture. In some cases, tools like spreadsheets and databases will be pressed into service to help capture the nuances of a complex architecture.

But the major documentation tool for information architecture or interaction design is the diagram. Representing the structure visually is the most efficient way for us to communicate the branches, groups, and interrelationships among the components of our site. Web site structures are inherently complicated things; trying to convey this complexity in words pretty much guarantees that no one will read them.

In the early days of the Web, this kind of diagram was called a "site map"; but because site map is also a term used for a particular kind of navigational tool on a site (which you'll read more about in Chapter 6), **architecture diagram** is now the favored term for the tool we use internally to describe site structure.

The diagram doesn't have to document every link on every page in your site. In fact, in most cases that level of detail only serves to confuse and obscure the information the team really needs. It's more important to document conceptual relationships: Which categories go together, and which remain separate? How do the steps in a given interaction sequence fit together?

The system I created to diagram site structures is called the Visual Vocabulary. Since I first posted it to the Web in 2000, information architects and interaction designers all over the world have adopted it. You can learn more about the Visual Vocabulary, see sample diagrams, and download tools for using it at my Web site: **www.jjg.net/ia/visvocab/**.

The Visual Vocabulary
is a system for
diagramming architec-
tures ranging from the
very simple (top) to the
very complex (bottom).
See **www.jjg.net/ia/
visvocab/** for more
details.

Because both interaction design and information architecture are relatively recent arrivals on the user experience landscape, it's still very common for Web development teams to have no one explicitly charged with responsibility for these areas. In light of this, it might not be all that surprising that so few Web sites display evidence that their structures were planned in advance.

Responsibility for structure often lands in someone's lap by default rather than through conscious planning. Who ends up responsible for structure often depends on the culture of the organization or the nature of the project. Early in the history of the Web, sites were usually created and managed by the organization's existing technical staff; in organizations where change happens slowly (or resources are very limited), this is likely to still be the case today.

For content-heavy sites or in organizations in which creating a presence on the Web was initially seen as a marketing activity, the responsibility for determining the structure of the site has resided within content development, editorial, or marketing communications groups. If the organization has historically been led by technical people or had a technology-oriented internal culture, responsibility for structure has commonly fallen to the technical project manager working on the Web site.

Every project can benefit from having a full-time specialist dedicated to structural issues. Sometimes this person goes by the job title "interaction designer," but more often they are likely to be referred to as an "information architect." Don't let the title confuse you—although it's true that some information architects specialize exclusively in creating organizational schemes and navigational structures for content sites, more often than not, an information architect will have some degree of experience with interaction design issues. In fact, some people who have held the title of information architect are really much closer to being interaction design specialists.

Your organization might not have the volume of ongoing work to warrant hiring a full-time information architect as a permanent member of your staff. If your Web development efforts are mostly limited to keeping the content you have up-to-date and you don't do much new development between site-wide redesign projects every couple of years, having a staff architect probably isn't a good way to spend your money. But if you have a steady stream of new content and functionality being added to your site, having an information architect on hand can help you manage that process in the way that will be most effective for meeting the needs of your users and for meeting your own strategic objectives.

Whether you have a specialist to address structural concerns isn't important, but it is important that those concerns are addressed by someone. Your site will have a structure whether you plan it out or not. The sites that are built according to a defined, explicit structural plan tend to be the ones that require less frequent overhauls, produce concrete results for their owners, and satisfy the needs of their users.

Further Reading

Cooper, Alan. *The Inmates Are Running the Asylum: Why High-Tech Products Drive Us Crazy and How to Restore the Sanity*. Sams, 1999.

Norman, Donald A. *The Design of Everyday Things*. Revised edition. Currency/Doubleday, 1990.

Rosenfeld, Louis and Peter Morville. *Information Architecture for the World Wide Web*. 2nd edition. O'Reilly, 2002.

Web resources: **www.jjg.net/elements/resources/**.

chapter 6

The Skeleton Plane

Interface Design, Navigation
Design, and Information Design

The conceptual structure begins to give shape to the mass of requirements arising from our strategic objectives. On the skeleton plane, we further refine that structure, identifying specific aspects of interface, navigation, and information design that will make the intangible structure concrete.

Surface

Skeleton

Structure

Scope

Strategy

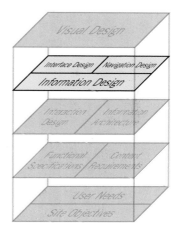

Defining the Skeleton

The structure plane covered in the preceding chapter defines how our site will work; the skeleton plane defines what form that functionality will take. In addition to addressing more concrete issues of presentation, the skeleton plane also deals with matters that involve a more refined level of detail. On the structure plane, we looked at the large-scale issues of architecture and interaction; on the skeleton plane, our concerns exist almost exclusively at the level of individual pages and their components.

On the software side, we define the skeleton through **interface design**—the familiar realm of buttons, fields, and other interface components. But information spaces have a unique set of problems all their own. **Navigation design** is the specialized form of interface design tailored to presenting information spaces. Finally, crossing both sides, we have **information design**, the presentation of information for effective communication.

Web as software interface	Web as hypertext system

skeleton

Interface Design | Navigation Design

Information Design

surface

↑
↓

structure

These three elements are closely bound together—more so than any of the other elements covered in this book. It's not uncommon to be faced with interface design problems that begin to blur into information design problems, or to encounter questions about information design that turn out to be matters of navigation design.

Even though the lines sometimes get blurry, identifying these as separate areas of concern helps us better assess whether we've settled on a suitable solution. Good navigation design can't correct bad information design; if we can't tell the difference between the types of problems, we can't tell if we've really solved them.

If it involves providing users with the ability to *do things*, it's interface design. The interface is the means by which users actually come into contact with the functionality defined in the specifications and structured in the interaction design.

If it involves providing users with the ability to *go places*, it's navigation design. The information architecture applied a structure to the list of content requirements we developed; the navigation design is the lens through which the user can see that structure, and is the means by which the user can move through it.

If it involves *communicating ideas* to the user, it's information design. This is the broadest of the three elements on this plane, potentially incorporating or drawing upon aspects of almost everything we've seen so far on both the software interface side and the hypertext information system side. Information design crosses the boundary between task-oriented software systems and information-oriented hypertext systems because neither interface design nor navigation design can be fully successful without good information design to support them.

Convention and Metaphor

Habit and reflex are the foundation for much of our interaction with the world—indeed, if we weren't able to reduce so much of what we do to reflex, we'd accomplish a whole lot less every day. Can you imagine if driving a car never got any easier than it was the first time you tried it? Your ability to drive, cook a meal, or use a computer—without being thoroughly exhausted by the tremendous concentration needed for the task—depends on the accumulation of lots of tiny reflexes.

Convention allows us to apply those reflexes in different circumstances. I used to have a car that invariably caused trouble whenever any of my friends drove it. When they started the car, the first thing they did was wash the windshield. This wasn't because they thought the windshield was dirty (though it probably was); rather, it was because they were trying to turn on the headlights. The controls on my car were different from the conventions they were used to.

Telephones are another good example of the importance of convention. From time to time, manufacturers have experimented with deviations from the standard three-by-four layout for the buttons on a telephone, such as two rows of six buttons each, or three rows of four. Circular arrangements still pop up from time to time, but these are becoming ever more rare as the rotary-dial phones on which they are based fade into the mists of technological oblivion.

It seems like the layout shouldn't make that much of a difference, but it does. If you measured the time a user spends trying to figure out which button to push on a nonstandard telephone, it might turn out to be something like three seconds per call. Not that big a difference—but to the user, those three seconds aren't just lost time. Those three seconds are filled with pure frustration, as a reflexive task becomes agonizingly slow simply because the rug of convention has been pulled out from under the user's feet.

In fact, the telephone's three-by-four matrix of digits is so well ingrained that it has become the standard for other devices that have nothing to do with telephones, such as microwave ovens or remote controls for televisions and VCRs. (Interestingly, the phone pad is not the only standard in this area: The "10-key" standard used by old adding machines, which inverts the order of the digits on the telephone keypad, can now be seen on calculators, computer keyboards, ATMs, cash registers, and in specialized data-entry applications such as inventory systems. Because both standards use a three-by-four matrix, people can adapt to either with relative ease, though a single standard would really be the best solution of all.)

This is not to say that the answer to every interface problem is slavish adherence to convention. Instead, you should simply be cautious about deviating from convention and only do so when a different approach offers clear benefits. Creating a successful user experience requires having explicitly defined reasons for every choice that you make.

Making your interface consistent with others that your users are already familiar with is important, but even more important is making your interface consistent with itself. The conceptual models for the features of your site can help you ensure internal consistency. If you have two features that both have the same conceptual model, they are likely to have similar interface requirements. Using the same conventions in both places allows a user who is familiar with one to adapt quickly to the other.

Even where the conceptual models for features differ, ideas that apply across a variety of conceptual models should be treated similarly (if not identically) wherever they appear. Concepts like "start," "finish," "go back," or "save" can be found in a wide range of contexts. Giving these a consistent treatment throughout lets users apply what they already know from having used other parts of the system, getting them to their goals faster and with fewer mistakes.

Just as you shouldn't take the conceptual models underlying your interaction design too literally, you should resist the impulse to construct your site around a series of **metaphors**. Metaphors for the features of your site are cute and fun, but they almost never work as well as it seems they should. In fact, they often don't work at all.

In some cases, you might be inclined to pattern the interface design for a particular function after the interface of a real-world object. Remember Slate's navigation in which you could "turn" the pages just like in a real magazine? Most interfaces and navigational devices in the real world are the product of the constraints of the real world: physics, the properties of materials, and so on. The Web has few of the same constraints.

Drawing analogies between features of your site and experiences people have in the real world might seem like a good way to help people get a handle on what those features are all about. However, this kind of approach usually obscures the nature of the feature instead of revealing it. Even though the association between the feature and its metaphorical representation is clear to you, it's just one of any number of associations your users might apply—especially if those users come from a different cultural background than you do. What does that little picture of a telephone mean? Can I make a phone call from this site? Check my voice mail? Pay my phone bill?

Of course, the content of your site should provide some degree of context to help users make better guesses about what features your metaphors are intended to represent. But the more diverse the range of content and functionality you offer, the less reliable these guesses become—and at any rate, some part of your audience is always going to guess incorrectly. It would be better (and simpler) to eliminate the user's guesswork altogether.

Avoiding metaphors is really just about reducing the mental effort required for users to get around and use the functionality of your site. Having an icon of a phone book to represent an actual directory of telephone numbers might be just fine; having a picture of a coffee shop to represent your chat area is a bit more problematic.

Interface Design

Successful interfaces are those in which users immediately notice the important stuff. Unimportant stuff, on the other hand, doesn't get noticed—sometimes because it's not there at all. One of the biggest challenges of designing interfaces for complex systems is figuring out which aspects the users don't need to deal with and reducing their visibility (or leaving them out altogether).

For people with a background in programming, this way of thinking can require some adjustment. It's often very different from what they are used to. Good programmers always take into account the most unlikely scenarios (called "edgecases" in programming jargon). After all, the ultimate accomplishment for programmers is creating software that never breaks; but programming that doesn't account for edgecases is likely to do exactly that under those extreme circumstances. So programmers are trained to treat every case equally, whether it represents one user or one thousand.

This approach doesn't work for interface design. An interface that gives a small number of extreme cases the same weight as the needs of the vast majority of users ends up ill-equipped to make either audience happy. A well-designed interface recognizes the courses of action users are most likely to take and makes those interface elements easiest to access and use.

This doesn't mean that the solution to every interface problem is to make the button users are most likely to push the biggest one on the page. Interface designs can employ a variety of tricks to ease users along the way to their goals. One simple trick is to think carefully about the default options selected when the interface is first presented to the user. If your understanding of your users' tasks and goals leads you to think most of them would prefer detailed search results over brief ones, leaving the "Show Me More Detail" checkbox checked by default means more people will automatically be happy with what they get, regardless of whether they took the time to read the label on the checkbox and make a decision for themselves. (Even better is a system that automatically remembers the options a user selected the last time they stopped by, but this sometimes requires more technical acrobatics than would appear necessary on the surface, and as a result is impractical for some development teams to implement successfully.)

The two primary technologies through which interfaces are delivered on the Web, HTML and Flash, have inherent technical constraints that limit the interface options available to us. This is actually both bad and good. It's bad because it limits our opportunities for innovation—some interface approaches that might be possible with traditional desktop software are simply impossible to realize on the Web. But this situation is also good, because users who learn how to work with a fairly small set of standard controls can apply that knowledge across a wide range of sites.

Although HTML was originally intended for simple hypertext information, people quickly saw its potential to provide more interactivity. Not long after its release into the world, HTML acquired a handful of standard interface elements:

Checkboxes allow users to select options independently of one another.

☐ **Checkboxes are independent**
☑ **So they can come in groups**

☐ **Or stand alone**

Radio buttons allow users to select one option from among a set of mutually exclusive options.

○ **Radio buttons**
○ **Come in groups**
○ **And are used to make**
◉ **Mutually exclusive selections**
○ **Burma-Shave**

Text fields allow users to—wait for it—enter text.

Text input fields let you input text

Dropdown lists provide the same functionality as radio buttons, but they do so in a more compact space, allowing many more options to be presented efficiently.

List boxes provide the same functionality as checkboxes, but they do so in a more compact space (because list boxes scroll). As with dropdowns, this enables the list box to easily support a large number of options.

Action buttons can do lots of different things. Typically, they tell the system to take all the other information the user has provided via other interface elements and do something—take action—with it.

Flash provides the same set of basic elements, but because of its origins as an animation tool, it can offer a greater degree of flexibility in how the interface can respond to the user. Consequently, Flash interfaces involve a lot more choices to be made during the design process, and they tend to be harder to get right.

Juggling all the different interface elements and choosing from among them inevitably involves tradeoffs. True, that dropdown will save you some space on the page relative to a set of radio buttons, but it will also hide the available choices from the user. Having people type in the categories they want to search might put less load on the database, but it puts more load on the user; if there are only six to choose from anyway, maybe some checkboxes would be better.

Interface design for the Web is all about selecting the right interface elements for the task the user is trying to accomplish and arranging them on the page in a way that will be readily understood and easily used. Tasks on Web sites will typically stretch across several pages, each containing a different set of interface elements for the user to contend with. Which functions end up on which pages is a matter of interaction design down in the structure plane; how those functions are realized on the page is the realm of interface design.

Dropdown lists can hinder users by hiding important options from view (left). Radio buttons easily display all the available options (right), but they take more space in the interface.

Additional options:

Additional options:

Additional options:

○ **gift wrap**
○ **pancakes**
◉ **a pony**

Information design plays a role in interface design problems when the interface must not only gather information from the user, but communicate information to the user as well. Error messages are a classic information design problem in creating successful interfaces; providing instructional information is another one, if only because the biggest challenge is getting users to actually read the instructions. Any time the system has to give the users some information for them to use the interface successfully—whether it's because they made a mistake or because they're just getting started—that's an information design problem.

Navigation Design

Navigation design seems like a simple business: Put links on every page that allow users to get around on the site. If you scratch the surface, however, the complexities of navigation design become apparent. The navigation design of any site must accomplish three simultaneous goals:

> ▶ First, it must provide users with a means for getting from one point to another on the site. Because it's usually impractical (and even when practical, it's generally not a good idea) to link to every page from every other page, navigation elements have to be selected to facilitate real user behavior—and by the way, that means those links have to actually work, too.

> ▶ Second, the navigation design must communicate the relationship between the elements it contains. It's not enough to merely provide a list of links. What do those links have to do with each other? Are some more important than others? What are the relevant differences between them? This communication is necessary for users to understand what choices are available to them.

> ▶ Third, the navigation design must communicate the relationship between its contents and the page the user is currently viewing. What does any of this stuff have to do with what I'm looking at right now? Communicating this helps users understand which of the available choices might best support the task or goal they are pursuing.

In a physical space, people can rely on some degree of an innate sense of direction to orient themselves. (Of course, some people just seem to be perpetually lost.) But the mechanisms in our brain that help us find our way around in the physical world ("Let's see, I think the entrance where I came in should be behind me and to the left") are utterly useless in helping us find our way around in an information space.

That's why it's of vital importance that every page of a Web site communicate clearly to users where they are on the site and where they can go. The question of to what extent users orient themselves in information spaces is currently a matter of some debate: Some people strongly favor the notion that users make little maps in their heads when they visit Web sites, just as they do in hardware stores and libraries; others claim users rely almost entirely on the navigational and wayfinding cues in front of them, as if each step they took through the site faded from their memory shortly after they took it.

We still don't know just how (or how much) people keep the struc-ture of Web sites in their heads. Until we figure it out, the best approach is to assume that users carry no knowledge with them from page to page. (After all, if a public search engine such as Google indexes your site, any page could be an entry point to your site anyway.)

Most sites actually provide multiple **navigation systems**, each ful-filling a particular role in enabling the user to navigate the site suc-cessfully in a variety of circumstances. Several common types of navigation systems have sprung up in practice.

Global navigation provides access to the broad sweep of the entire site. The use of the term "global" here doesn't necessarily imply that this navigation appears on every page in the site—although that's not a bad idea. (We use the term "persistent" to refer to navigation elements that appear throughout a site; again, keep in mind that persistent elements are not necessarily global.) Instead, global navi-gation brings together the key set of access points that users might need to get from one end of the site to the other. Anywhere you might want to go, you can get there (eventually) from the global navigation.

Global navigation.

Local navigation provides users with access to what's "nearby" in the architecture. In a strictly hierarchical architecture, local navigation might provide access to a page's parent, siblings, and children. If your architecture is constructed to reflect the ways users think about the site's content, local navigation will typically get more use than other navigation systems.

Local navigation.

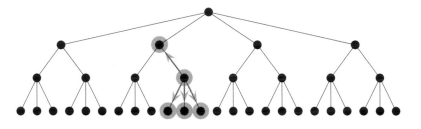

Supplementary navigation provides shortcuts to related content that might not be readily accessible through the global or local navigation. This type of navigation scheme offers some of the benefits of faceted classification (allowing users to shift the focus of their exploration of the content without starting over at the beginning), while still permitting the site to maintain a primarily hierarchical architecture.

Supplementary
navigation.

Contextual navigation (sometimes called "inline navigation") is embedded in the content of the page itself. This type of navigation— for example, a hyperlink within the text of a page—often goes under- (or mis-) utilized. Often, the moment when users decide they need a different piece of information is when they're reading the text. Instead of forcing your users to scan the page for the right navigation element—or worse, sending them scurrying to the search engine—why not put the relevant link right there?

Reaching all the way back to the strategy plane, the better you understand your users and their needs, the more effectively you can deploy contextual navigation. If it doesn't clearly support your users' tasks and goals—if your text is crammed full of so many hyperlinks that users can't pick out what's relevant to their needs—contextual navigation will (rightly) be seen as clutter.

Contextual navigation.

Courtesy navigation.

Courtesy navigation provides access to items that users don't need on a regular basis, but that are commonly provided as a convenience. In the physical world, a retail store will usually post its hours of operation at its entrance. For most customers, most of the time, this information isn't all that helpful: Anybody can tell pretty quickly whether or not the shop is open for business. But knowing that the information is readily available helps them when they do need it. Links to contact information, feedback forms, and policy statements are commonly found in courtesy navigation.

Some navigational devices aren't embedded within the structure of your pages, but stand on their own, independent of the content or functionality of your site. These are **remote navigation** tools that users turn to most often when they get frustrated with the other navigational systems you've provided, or when they've taken one look at your navigational systems and quickly come to the conclusion that they're better off not even attempting to figure them out.

A **site map** is a common remote navigation tool that gives users a concise, one-page snapshot of the overall site architecture. The site map is usually presented as a hierarchical "outline" of the site, providing links to all the top-level sections with links to major second-level sections indented beneath them. Site maps don't usually show more than two levels of the hierarchy—beyond that is more detail than users typically need (and if it isn't, there's probably something wrong with your high-level architecture).

An **index** is an alphabetical list of topics with links to relevant pages, much like the index in the back of a book. This type of tool is most effective for sites that have a great deal of content covering a diverse range of subjects. In most other cases, a site map and a well-planned architecture should be sufficient. Indexes are sometimes developed for individual sections of a site, rather than attempting to cover the entire sweep of the site's content; this approach can be useful when you have sections intended to serve different audiences with divergent information needs.

Information Design

Information design can sometimes be difficult to put your finger on. It often serves as the glue that holds the other components of the design together. In all cases, information design comes down to making decisions about *how to present information* so that people can use it or understand it more easily.

Sometimes information design is visual. Is a pie chart the best way to present that data, or would a bar chart work better for our users? Does the "binoculars" icon adequately convey the concept of searching the site, or would a magnifying glass be better understood?

Sometimes information design involves grouping or arranging pieces of information. We often take this aspect of design for granted because we are used to seeing common information grouped in certain ways. For example, look at this list of items:

▶ State

▶ Job title

▶ Telephone number

▶ Street address

▶ Name

▶ Zip code

▶ Organization

▶ City

▶ E-mail address

It seems a little confusing, because usually it looks more like this:

▶ Name

▶ Job title

▶ Organization

▶ Street address

▶ City

▶ State

▶ Zip code

▶ Telephone number

▶ E-mail address

Even this arrangement could be clarified further:

- ▶ Personal information
  - ▶ Name
  - ▶ Job title
  - ▶ Organization
- ▶ Address information
  - ▶ Street address
  - ▶ City
  - ▶ State
  - ▶ Zip code
- ▶ Other contact information
  - ▶ Telephone number
  - ▶ E-mail address

This example seems pretty straightforward, but a slightly different list of items could prove more challenging:

- ▶ Power limit
- ▶ Rotor size
- ▶ Tank capacity
- ▶ Transmission type
- ▶ Median angular velocity
- ▶ Chassis style
- ▶ Maximum output

The key, of course, is to group and arrange the information elements in ways that reflect how your users think and support their tasks and goals. The conceptual relationships between these elements really amount to micro-level information architecture; information design comes into play when we have to *communicate* that structure on the page.

Wayfinding

One important function that information design and navigation design work together to perform is supporting **wayfinding**. The idea of wayfinding comes from the design of public spaces in the physical world. Parks, stores, roads, airports, and parking lots all benefit from the incorporation of wayfinding devices. Parking garages, for example, will sometimes use color coding to give people cues to help them remember where they left their cars. In airports, signs, maps, and other indicators help people find their way around.

On Web sites, wayfinding typically involves both navigation design and information design. The navigation systems employed by a site not only have to provide access to the different areas of the site, they also have to communicate those choices successfully. Good wayfinding enables users to quickly get a mental picture of where they are, where they can go, and which choices will get them closer to their objectives.

The information design component of wayfinding involves page elements that don't perform a navigational function. For example, just like in parking garages, some Web sites have been very successful in using color-coding to indicate which section a user is looking at. (However, color-coding is almost never used by itself—instead, it reinforces another wayfinding system also in place.) Icons, labeling systems, and typography are other information design systems sometimes used to help reinforce a sense of "you are here" for users.

Wireframes

Page layout is where information design, interface design, and navigation design come together to form a unified, cohesive skeleton. The page layout must incorporate all the various navigation systems, each designed to convey a different view of the architecture; all the interface elements required by any functionality on the page; and the information design that supports both of these, as well as the information design of the page content itself.

It's a lot to balance all at once. That's why page layout is covered in detail in a document called a page schematic or **wireframe**. The wireframe is a bare-bones depiction (as the name suggests) of all the components of a page and how they fit together.

Wireframes capture all the skeleton decisions in a single document that serves as a reference for visual design work and site implementation. Wireframes can contain varying levels of detail—this one is pretty light.

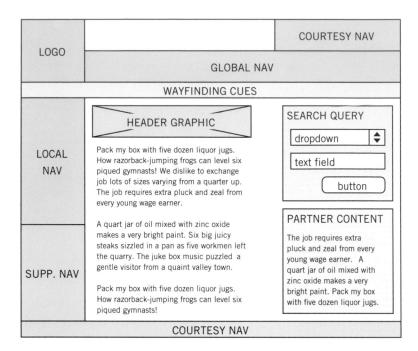

This simple line drawing is usually heavily annotated, referring the reader to architecture diagrams or other interaction design documentation, content requirements or functional specifications, or other types of detailed documentation as needed. For example, if a wireframe refers to specific existing content elements, it might provide pointers to where they can be found. In addition, the wireframe will often contain supplementary notes on intended site behavior that might not be obvious from just looking at the wireframe and the architecture diagram.

In many ways, the architecture diagram we saw back in the structure plane is the grand vision for the project; here in the skeleton plane, the wireframe is the detailed document that shows just how that vision will be fulfilled. Wireframes will sometimes be supplemented by comprehensive navigational specifications, describing in more detail the precise composition of each of the various navigational components.

For smaller or less complex sites, a single wireframe is sufficient to serve as a template for all the pages that will be built. For many projects, however, multiple wireframes are needed to convey the complexity of the intended result. You probably won't need a wireframe for each page of the site, however. Just as the architectural process allowed us to classify content elements into broad classes, a relatively small number of standard page types will emerge from wireframe development.

Wireframes are a necessary first step in the process of formally establishing the visual design for the site, but almost everyone involved in the development process will use them at some point. People responsible for strategy, scope, and structure can refer to the wireframe to confirm that the final product will meet their expectations. People responsible for actually building the site can refer to the wireframe to answer questions about how the site should function.

As the field of user experience development has grown and evolved, responsibility for the wireframe has at times been the subject of a sort of turf war inside organizations. Some Web development teams are highly compartmentalized to the point that they have distinct roles (and sometimes entire departments!) for "information architects" and "designers."

The wireframe, being the place where information architecture and visual design come together, then becomes a subject of debate and dispute. Information architects complain that designers who create wireframes obscure their architectures behind navigation systems that don't reflect the principles underlying the architectures. Visual designers complain that wireframes produced by information architects reduce their role to that of paint-by-numbers artist, squandering the experience and expertise in visual communication they bring to information design problems.

When you have separate information architects and designers, the only way to produce successful wireframes is through collaboration. The process of having to work out the details of the wireframe together enables each side to see issues from the other's point of view, and it can help uncover problems early in the process (instead of later, when the site is being built and everyone is wondering why it isn't working as planned).

All of this makes wireframes sound like a whole lot of work. They don't have to be. Documentation is never an end in itself; it is only a means to an end. Creating documentation for its own sake is not merely a waste of time—it can be counter-productive and demoralizing. Producing the right level of documentation for your needs—and not fooling yourself that you can get by with less—turns documentation from a problem into an advantage.

Some of the most successful wireframes I've ever worked with have been nothing more than pencil sketches with Post-It Notes attached. For a small team in which the designer and the programmer sit right next to each other, that level of documentation is perfectly sufficient. But when programming is the responsibility of an entire team and not just one person—and that team is halfway around the world—something a bit more formal is probably called for.

The value of wireframes is the way they integrate all three elements of the structure plane: interface design, through the arrangement and selection of interface elements; navigation design, through the identification and definition of core navigational systems; and information design, through the placement and prioritization of informational components. By bringing all three together into a single document, the wireframe can define a skeleton that builds on the underlying conceptual structure while pointing the way forward toward visual design.

Further Reading

Fleming, Jennifer. *Web Navigation: Designing the User Experience*. O'Reilly, 1998.

Spolsky, Joel. *User Interface Design for Programmers*. Apress, 2001.

Tufte, Edward. *Envisioning Information*. Graphics Press, 1990.

Veen, Jeffrey. *The Art & Science of Web Design*. New Riders, 2000.

Web resources: **www.jjg.net/elements/resources/**.

chapter **7**

The Surface Plane

Visual Design

At the top of the five-plane model, we turn our

attention to those aspects of the site our users will

notice first: the visual design. Here, content, func-

tionality, and aesthetics come together to produce

a finished design that fulfills all the goals of the

other four planes.

Surface

Skeleton

Structure

Scope

Strategy

Defining the Surface

On the skeleton plane, we were dealing primarily with arrangement. Interface design concerns the arrangement of elements to enable interaction, navigation design concerns the arrangement of elements to enable movement through the site, and information design concerns the arrangement of elements to communicate information to the user.

Moving up to the surface plane, we are now dealing with the visual presentation of the logical arrangements that make up the skeleton of the site. For example, through attention to information design, we determine how we should group and arrange the information elements of the page; through attention to **visual design**, we determine how that arrangement should be presented visually.

Initially, you might think visual design is a simple matter of aesthetics. Everybody has different taste, and everybody has a different idea of what constitutes a visually appealing design, so every argument over design decisions just comes down to personal preference, right? Well, everybody does have a different sense of aesthetics, but that doesn't mean design decisions have to be based on what looks "cool" to everyone involved.

Instead of evaluating visual design ideas solely in terms of what seems aesthetically pleasing, you should focus your attention on how well they work. How effectively does the design support the objectives defined by each of the lower planes? Does the look of the site undermine the structure, making distinctions between sections of the architecture unclear or ambiguous? Or does the visual design reinforce the structure, clarifying the options available to users?

Communicating a brand identity, for example, is a common strategic objective for a Web site. Brand identity comes across in many ways—in the language you use or in the interaction design of your site's functionality—but one of the main tools used to communicate brand identity is visual design. If the identity you want to convey is technical and authoritative, using comic-book fonts and bright pastel colors probably isn't the right choice. It's not just a matter of aesthetics, it's a matter of strategy.

Follow the Eye

One simple way to to evaluate the visual design of a page is to ask: Where does the eye go first? What element of the design initially draws the user's attention? Are they drawn to something important to the site's strategic objectives? Or is the first object of their attention a distraction from their goals (or yours)?

Researchers sometimes use sophisticated **eyetracking** equipment to determine exactly what test subjects are looking at and how their eyes move about the page. If you're just fine-tuning the visual design of a page, however, you can usually get away with simply asking people—even just asking yourself. Sometimes this approach won't provide the most accurate results, and it will never capture all the nuances that eyetracking equipment can provide. But most of the time, simply asking questions is perfectly suitable. Another way to find the dominant design element is to squint at the page or blur your eyes until you can't make out the details—or walk to the other end of the room and look at it from there.

Then try to determine where the eye goes. If you're serving as your own test subject, pay attention to the unconscious movements of your eyes around the page. Don't think too much about what you're looking at; just let your eyes take in the page naturally. If someone else is your test subject, ask them to call out the elements of the page in the order that their attention is drawn to them.

Generally, you'll find that people follow fairly consistent patterns in how their eyes move across the page—after all, these are largely unconscious, instinctive eye movements. If subjects report their eyes following a very different pattern from other people, they probably aren't really aware of their natural eye movements, or they're just telling you what they think you want to hear (or both).

If your design is successful, the pattern the user's eye follows around the page will have two important qualities:

▶ First, it follows a smooth flow. When people comment that a design is "busy" or "cluttered," they're really reacting to the fact that the design doesn't lead them smoothly around the page. Instead, their eyes bounce back and forth among a variety of elements all clamoring for their attention.

▶ Second, it gives users a sort of "guided tour" of the possibilities available to them without overwhelming them with detail. As always, those possibilities should support the goals and tasks the user is trying to accomplish. Perhaps more importantly, those possibilities shouldn't distract from information or functions that users will need to fulfill those goals.

The movement of the user's eyes around the page doesn't happen by accident. It's the result of a complex set of deeply ingrained instinctive responses to visual stimuli that all humans share. Fortunately for us designers, these responses are not completely outside our control either—over the centuries, we've developed a variety of effective visual techniques for attracting and directing attention.

In a visually neutral layout (top left), nothing stands out. Contrast can be used to guide the user's eye around the page (top right) or draw their attention to a few key elements (bottom left). Overuse of contrast leads to a cluttered look (bottom right).

Contrast and Uniformity

In visual design, the primary tool we use to draw the user's attention is **contrast**. A design without contrast is seen as a gray, featureless mass, causing the user's eyes to drift around without settling on anything in particular. Contrast is vital to drawing the user's attention to essential aspects of the interface, contrast helps the user understand the relationships between the navigational elements on the page, and contrast is the primary means of communicating conceptual groups in information design.

When elements in a design are different, users pay attention. They can't help it. You can use this instinctive behavior to your advantage by making the pieces users really need to see stand out from the rest of the elements on the page. Error messages in Web interfaces often suffer from blending in with the rest of the page; contrasting them by putting the text in a different color (like, say, red) or highlighting them with a bold graphic can make all the difference.

For this strategy to work, however, the difference has to be significant enough for the user to clearly tell that the design choice is intended to communicate something. When the design treatment of two elements is similar but not quite the same, users get confused. "Why are those different? Are they supposed to be the same? Maybe it was just a mistake. Or am I supposed to notice something here?" Instead, we want both to grab users' attention and to assure them that it was intentional.

Maintaining **uniformity** in your design is an important part of ensuring that your design communicates effectively without confusing or overwhelming your users. Uniformity comes into play in many different aspects of visual design.

Keeping the sizes of elements uniform can make it easier to recombine them into new designs as you need them. For example, if all the graphic buttons you use for navigation are the same height, they can be mixed and matched as needed without creating a cluttered layout or requiring that new graphics be produced.

Grid-based layout is one technique from print design that carries over effectively to the Web. This approach ensures uniformity of design through a "master layout" that is used as a template for creating layout variations. Not every layout will use every part of the grid—in fact, most layouts will probably only use a few—but every element's placement on the grid should be uniform and consistent. However, because Web browsers don't afford complete control of the size of text elements, applying grids to the Web isn't always as simple as it is in print design.

Creating a grid to guide layout work enables uniformity without sacrificing consistency.

It's easy to fall into the trap of adhering to a grid system—or any standard intended to ensure uniformity—even when it clearly isn't working anymore. The anarchy of working without design standards is bad, but the straitjacket of trying to work within design standards that are inadequate for your needs can be worse. Maybe the site has taken on new functionality that no one had imagined at the time when the grid was developed; maybe the grid just never worked all that well in the first place. Whatever the reason, it's important to be able to recognize when it's time to revisit the foundations of your design system.

Internal and External Consistency

Because of the way Web sites often have been produced—piecemeal, ad-hoc, and isolated from other design work going on in the organization—they have been plagued with problems of consistency in visual design. These problems take two forms:

- ▶ First, there are problems of internal consistency, in which different parts of the site reflect different design approaches.

- ▶ Then there are problems of external consistency, in which the site doesn't reflect the same design approach used in other products from the same organization.

Good solutions to problems of internal consistency are rooted in an understanding of the skeleton of the site. Identify recurring design elements that appear in different contexts throughout the various interface, navigation, and information design problems on the site. By removing each design element from those different contexts before we design it, we can more clearly see the small-scale problem we're trying to solve, instead of getting distracted by the larger-scale problems imposed by context. Rather than designing the same element over and over again, we can examine it in isolation, design it once, and use that design throughout the site.

Obviously, for such an approach to work, we will still have to check our work against the different contexts in which that element appears. Maybe a big, round, red "STOP" button will work fine for the checkout page, but it might not work so well on the crowded product customization page. The best approach is to isolate each element, design it, try the design in various contexts, and then rework the design as needed.

Even though many of the design elements will be created in isolation from each other, they should still work together. A successful design is not merely a collection of small, well-designed objects; rather, the objects should form a *system* that operates as a cohesive, consistent whole.

Historically, problems of internal consistency often came about because many Web sites grew out of corporate IT departments, which generally had little understanding of (and even less access to) company visual design standards. In the early days, this divide was only reinforced by the profound technical limitations that the new medium placed on design. Marketing departments, accustomed to the nearly infinite control afforded by designing for print and broadcast media, essentially disowned Web design as being too primitive to be worth their resources. IT departments, left to their own devices, learned to accommodate the limits of the new medium and gradually developed their own design standards.

These days, however, most marketing departments have more direct control over the look of their companies' Web sites. Also, advances in technology and more sophisticated design techniques have enabled Web sites to look more like their print and broadcast counterparts than ever. As a result, sites sporting a radically different look from the rest of the material produced by their owners are growing increasingly rare.

You still can't expect to be able to do everything with Web design that you can do with design in other media. Nevertheless, you can gain a lot of value from making sure your online and offline styles align wherever possible. This doesn't mean that the styles must be precisely the same—instead, they should be constructed so as to produce the same effect.

Enforcing design consistency across media presents your audience—customers, prospects, shareholders, employees, or casual observers—with a uniform impression of your brand identity. This consistency of brand identity plays out at every level of the design of your site, from the navigation elements appearing across every page to the humble button that appears only once.

Presenting a style on your Web site that's inconsistent with your style in other media doesn't just affect the audience's impression of the site; it affects their impression of your company as a whole. People respond positively to companies with clearly defined identities. Inconsistent visual styles undermine the clarity of your corporate image and leave the audience with the impression that this is a company that hasn't quite figured out who it is.

Color Palettes and Typography

Color can be one of the most effective ways to communicate a brand identity. Some brands are so closely associated with colors that it's difficult to think of the company without the color automatically coming to mind—consider Coca-Cola, UPS, or Kodak. These companies have employed specific colors (red, brown, yellow) consistently over the years to create a stronger sense of their identities in the public's mind.

That doesn't mean they use these colors to the exclusion of all others. The core brand colors are usually part of a broader **color palette** used in all of a company's materials. The colors in a company's standard palette are selected specifically for how well they work together, complementing each other without competing.

A color palette should incorporate colors that lend themselves to a wide range of uses. In most cases, brighter or bolder colors can be used for the foreground of your design—elements to which you want to draw attention. More muted colors are better used for background elements that don't need to jump off the page. Having a range of colors to choose from provides us with a toolkit for making effective design choices.

Just as contrast and uniformity are important to other areas of visual design, they play a vital role in the creation of color palettes as well. When used in the same context, colors that are very close to one another, but not quite the same, undermine the effectiveness of your color palette. This doesn't mean you only get one shade of red, one shade of blue, and so forth. It means that if you want to use different shades of red, make sure they're different enough that users can tell them apart, and make sure you use each in consistent ways.

For some companies, **typography**—the use of fonts or typefaces to create a particular visual style—is so important to their brand identities that they have commissioned special typefaces to be produced specifically for their use. Organizations ranging from Apple Computer to Volkswagen to the London Underground have used custom typography to create a stronger sense of identity in their communications. But even if you choose not to take this extraordinary step, type can still serve as an effective part of communicating your identity through visual design.

Like many organiza-
tions, Apple Computer
uses consistent
typography—both on
its Web site and in
other media—to convey
a consistent brand
image.

Store   Switch   .Mac   QuickTime   Support   Mac OS X
Hot News   Hardware   Software   Made4Mac   Education   Creative   SmallBiz   Developer   Where to Buy

iMac.

How millions of new users get
on the Internet — in minutes.

With all the built-in hardware and software you need to get online, the
iMac is an expert at connecting to the Internet — so you don't have to
be.

This iMac gives you the same core functionality and ease of use that enabled
millions of iMac owners to enjoy their first experience of the Internet. Only
now, the entry-level iMac has more than twice the performance of the
original iMac, offers four times the hard disk capacity, four times as much
RAM — and costs $500 less.

The Apple Store offers
convenient online ordering
24 hours a day, every day.

You can't beat the system
With the advanced, yet easy-to-use Mac
OS X preinstalled on your iMac, you'll
work and play with the most rock-solid
— and reliable — OS technologies on the
planet.

**A million fans on the outside,
none on the inside**
The one thing you won't hear is a fan.
There isn't one. The iMac takes
advantage of a unique design feature to
cool itself quietly.

Buy
Now

What makes the iMac so special?

Connect

Tech Specs.
All you want to know about
CPU, memory, hard disk,
ports and more.

Software.
Every iMac includes a suite
of useful, powerful and fun
applications.

Internet.
Legendary for its ease of
use, the iMac gets you on the
Internet in minutes.

The iMac features a built-in 15-inch shadow-mask CRT display with three
crisp, super-sharp screen resolutions — perfect for editing text, viewing
graphics and playing games — and comes with 128MB of RAM. Plus 256K of
Level 2 cache running at full processor speed, ATI RAGE 128 Ultra graphics
accelerator with 16MB of dedicated SDRAM, built-in microphone, dual mini-
headphone jacks, dual FireWire ports and USB ports, a 10/100BASE-T
Ethernet port, 56K modem, and a slot for an AirPort Card. The hard disk is a

The 108-key Apple Pro Keyboard has a
built-in two-port USB hub and special
keys that let you adjust audio volume,
mute the speakers and even eject a CD
from the slot-loading drive. The
smooth-gliding Apple Pro Mouse uses a
high-precision optical sensor for
unparalleled accuracy.

Because of the limited resolution of computer screens, some typefaces that would be perfectly acceptable on paper can be very difficult to read on a Web site. For this reason, typefaces designed expressly to be highly readable on screen (such as Microsoft's Georgia and Verdana fonts) have become popular alternatives to less legible "default" fonts such as Arial or Times New Roman.

For larger text elements or short labels like those seen on navigational elements, typefaces with a little more personality are perfectly appropriate. But one of our objectives is not to overwhelm our users with visual clutter, and using an unnecessarily wide variety of fonts—or even using a small number of fonts in inconsistent ways—can contribute to that sense of clutter. In most cases, you won't need more than a handful of fonts to meet all your communication needs.

The principles of using type effectively are really the same as those for other aspects of visual design: Don't use styles that are very similar but not exactly the same. Use different styles only to indicate differences in the information you're trying to communicate. Provide enough contrast between styles that you can draw the user's attention as needed, but don't overload the design with a wide range of diverse styles.

Design Comps and Style Guides

The most direct analogue to the wireframe for the realm of visual design is the visual mock-up or **design comp**. The "comp" is short for composite, because that's exactly what it is: a visualization of the finished product built up from the components that have been chosen. The comp shows how all the pieces work together to form a cohesive whole; or, if they don't, it shows where the breakdown is happening and demonstrates constraints that any solution will have to account for.

You should be able to see a simple one-to-one correlation between components of the wireframe and components of the design comp. The comp might not faithfully reproduce the layout of the wireframe—in most cases it probably won't. The wireframe doesn't account for visual design concerns, focusing instead on documenting the skeleton. Building the wireframe before we tackle the design comp allows us to look at skeleton issues in isolation first, then see how surface issues come into play. Nevertheless, the conceptual aspects of the wireframe, particularly regarding information design issues, should be plainly evident in the design comps, even though they may not follow the precise arrangement presented in the wireframe.

The definitive documentation of all the design decisions we have made is the **style guide**. This compendium defines every aspect of the visual design, from the largest scale to the smallest. Global standards affecting every page of the site—such as design grids, color palettes, typography standards, or logo treatment guidelines—are usually the first things to go into a style guide.

The visual design doesn't have to match the wireframe precisely—it only has to account for the relative importance and grouping of elements presented in the wireframe.

The style guide will also include standards specific to a particular section or function of a site. In some cases, the standards documented in the style guide will go all the way down to the level of individual interface and navigation elements. The overall goal of the style guide is to provide enough detail to help people make smart decisions in the future (because most of the thinking has already been done for them).

All of this documentation is, of course, a lot of work, but it happens for a good reason: Over time, the reasons for our decisions fade from memory. The ad-hoc decisions made to address a specific problem in a specific circumstance get all jumbled up with the decisions intended to form the foundation for future design work.

Another reason to document your design system is that people eventually quit their jobs. When they do, they walk away with a wealth of knowledge about how a site gets designed and built on a day-to-day basis. Without a style guide that remains up-to-date with the latest standards and practices, that knowledge is lost. Over time, as people change positions, the whole organization gradually suffers a sort of amnesia, as the ways things were done and the reasons for those decisions drift away to other parts of the company or back out into the workforce.

Creating a style guide is also helpful in imposing design consistency across a decentralized organization. If your Web operations consist of a diverse range of independent projects being initiated and worked on by people in offices scattered all over the world, your site is likely to look like a random mish-mash of styles and standards. Getting all those people to go along with a unified set of standards can be a lot of work, which is why responsibility for enforcing design style guides often resides higher up in the organization than you might expect. A single style guide, designed to take the needs of all these different projects into account, is a big undertaking, but it's not impossible, and it's the single most effective way to get your Web site looking like a coherent whole instead of just a jumble of tacked-on pieces.

Further Reading

Mullet, Kevin and Darrell Sano. *Designing Visual Interfaces: Communication Oriented Techniques*. Prentice Hall, 1994.

Williams, Robin. *The Non-Designer's Design Book*. Peachpit, 1994.

Web resources: **www.jjg.net/elements/resources/**

chapter **8**

The Elements Applied

The elements of user experience remain consistent no matter how big your site is. But putting the ideas behind the elements into practice can sometimes seem like a challenge all by itself. It's not just a question of time and resources—it's often a question of mindset.

Looking back over the five planes—strategy, scope, structure, skeleton, and surface—it all sounds like a whole lot of work. Surely such careful attention to all these details must take months of development time and a small army of highly trained specialists, right?

Not necessarily. Certainly, for some projects and some organizations, employing a team of dedicated specialists is the most effective way to parcel out responsibility for a site that's simply too complex to handle any other way. Also, because specialists can focus exclusively on a subset of the complete user experience, they often bring a deeper understanding of those issues to bear in their work. Much of the time, however, small teams with limited resources can achieve similar results. Sometimes a group of just a few people can actually produce better results than a large team.

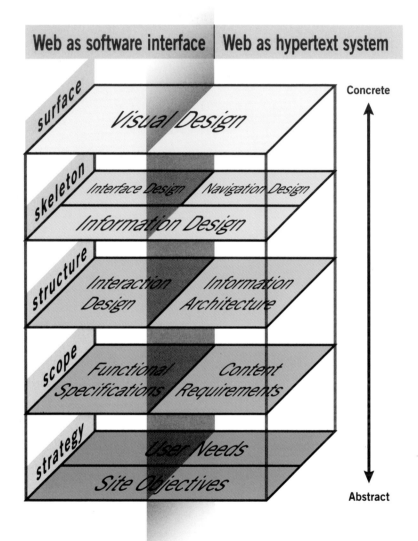

Creating the user experience is really little more than a very large collection of very small problems to be solved. The difference between a successful approach and one doomed to failure really comes down to two basic ideas:

- **Understand what problem you're trying to solve.** So you've worked out that the big purple button on the home page is a problem. Is it the bigness and the purpleness of the button that needs to change (surface)? Or is it that the button is in the wrong place on the page (skeleton) or that the function the button represents doesn't work the way users expect it to (structure)?

- **Understand the consequences of your solution to the problem.** Remember that there's a potential "ripple effect" up and down through the elements from every decision you make. The navigation design that works so well in one part of your site might not quite meet the needs of another section of the architecture. The interaction design for the product selection wizard might well be an innovative approach, but will it meet the needs of your technophobic users?

This might seem to be a painfully obvious approach to the task of creating the user experience of your site, but you'd be surprised at just how many of the tiny decisions that make up the user experience development process aren't made consciously at all. Most of the time, the choices made about the user experience fall into one of these scenarios:

▶ **Design by default.** This happens when the structure of the user experience follows the structure of the underlying technology or of your organization. Keeping the customer's order history and billing information in separate databases might work better for your existing technical system, but that doesn't mean keeping them separate in the user experience is also a good idea. Similarly, content that comes from different departments in the company might serve the user better if it were brought together, not kept separate.

▶ **Design by mimicry.** This happens when the user experience falls back on familiar conventions from other sites, publications, or software applications, regardless of how appropriate those conventions might be to your users (or even to the Web itself). The widespread, haphazard adoption of tabs as a global navigation device in the late 1990s is one example of this phenomenon.

▶ **Design by fiat.** This happens when personal preferences drive user experience decisions instead of user needs or site objectives. If orange dominates your color palette because one of the senior vice presidents is fond of it, or if all your navigational elements are drop-down menus because that's what your head engineer likes, you've lost sight of the strategic goals that should be driving the choices you make.

An Example: Search Engine Implementation

Search engines are probably the most common feature anywhere on the Web—everyone uses them at one time or another, and sites that don't offer search engines are increasingly rare. But even though they seem to be everywhere, these apparently simple tools require a complex set of decisions spanning every plane of the elements of user experience if they are to be implemented successfully.

The nearly ubiquitous inclusion of search engines on Web sites reflects the growing understanding that the capability to retrieve content matching specific criteria is a practically universal user need, regardless of the specific audience or content in question. Addressing this user need is a key **strategy** decision.

The site's content requirements and functional specifications dictate the **scope** of what the search engine can offer users. If having meta-data about your content is a requirement for the site, the search engine can provide users with enhanced capabilities that make use of that data, such as enabling them to search only for articles by a particular author or those published within a certain time period. If some of your metadata is not intended to be used by the search engine, the functional specifications can detail exactly what types of searches users can perform.

The search engine really starts to take shape when **structure** issues—interaction design and information architecture—are taken into consideration. The interaction design of the search function determines how users will actually work with the search engine. Perhaps the search functionality is so complex that it will require a lengthy, structured process before the user even gets to see results; on the other hand, maybe all you need is a keyword entry field on every page.

Also, if the search engine is aware of the information architecture of the site as a whole, it can offer more capabilities to the user, such as the option to restrict a search to one particular area of the site or to automatically sort search results according to their placement in the architecture. In addition, the search results will have an information architecture of their own. Do all results appear on a single page, or are they broken out across multiple pages? If the latter, how does the user get from one page to another? Can he jump around arbitrarily, or is he limited to a strictly sequential navigation path?

These structural decisions take concrete form in the **skeleton** of the search engine. The interaction design takes shape in the arrangement of buttons, fields, and other interface elements that enable the user to submit a query to the system. The information architecture is reflected in the design of the navigational elements that allow the user to move through search results. Throughout, information design shows users how to construct queries and enables them to scan through search results to find what they need.

On the **surface**, all these elements are bound together into a cohesive whole by the search engine's visual design, which gives interface and information elements alike a consistent look and draws attention to the areas of the page in which users are likely to be most interested (or that they would otherwise miss).

Asking the Right Questions

Facing the tangle of small problems to be solved in creating the user experience can sometimes be disheartening. Occasionally a solution to one problem will force you to rethink other problems you thought you had already solved. Many times, you will have to make compromises and evaluate tradeoffs between different approaches. When you're in the middle of having to make these kinds of decisions, it's easy to become frustrated and question whether you're taking the right approach. The simple fact is this: The right approach is one in which no aspect of the user's experience is left to chance. Make every decision consciously and deliberately and ground each decision in your understanding of the underlying issues at play.

Having the right frame of mind about approaching the problems you are facing matters most. Every other aspect of the user experience development process can be adjusted to fit the time, money, and people at your disposal. No time to gather market research data on your audience? Maybe you can find ways to look at the information you already have, such as server logs or feedback e-mails, to get a sense of the needs of your users. Can't afford to rent a usability test lab? Recruit friends, family, or co-workers to participate in informal testing.

The worst mistake you can make is to gloss over the fundamental user experience issues of the project in the name of saving time or money. On some projects, someone will thoughtfully tack on some form of user experience evaluation to the very end of the process— long after the time to actually address those issues has run out. Racing toward launch without looking back might have seemed like a good idea back when the launch date was set, but the result is likely to be a site that meets all the technical requirements for the project but doesn't work for your users. Even worse, by tacking user experience evaluation on at the end, you might end up launching a site that you know is broken but have no opportunity (or money left) to fix.

Some organizations favor this approach, calling it "user acceptance testing." The word "acceptance" is very telling here—the question is not whether they like the site or will use the site, but rather can they accept the site? This type of testing all too often happens at the very end of the process, by which time countless assumptions have gone into shaping the user experience without ever being examined. Those assumptions can be extraordinarily difficult to uncover in user testing, because they are hidden behind layers of interface and interaction.

Many people advocate user testing as the primary means of ensuring a good user experience. This line of thinking seems to be that you should make something, put it in front of some people to see how they like it, and then fix whatever they complained about. But testing is never a substitute for a thoughtful, informed user experience design process.

Questions that focus on specific elements of the user experience can help you gather more relevant input from your users. User tests constructed without an eye toward the elements of user experience can end up asking the wrong questions, which in turn can lead to the wrong answers. For example, when testing prototypes, knowing what problem you're setting out to investigate is crucial to presenting your test subjects with an experience that doesn't cloud the matter with unrelated issues. Is the problem with that navigation bar really just the color? Or is it the wording that your users are responding to?

You simply cannot depend on your users to articulate their needs. The challenge in creating any user experience is to understand the needs of the users better than they understand those needs themselves. Testing can help you understand the needs of your users, but it's just one of many tools that can help achieve the same end.

The Marathon and the Sprint

Just as you shouldn't leave any aspect of the user experience to chance, you shouldn't leave your own development process to chance either. Too many Web development teams operate in a state of permanent emergency. Each project is conceived as the response to some perceived crisis, and as a result, every project is behind schedule before it even begins.

I have a metaphor for the user experience development process that I often use when describing problems to clients: A marathon is not a sprint. Know which kind of race you're in and run accordingly.

A sprint is a short race. Sprinters have to call upon vast reserves of energy at the instant the starting gun is fired—and they expend all of that energy in the space of a few minutes. Right off the starting line, the sprinter has to run as fast as he can and keep running as fast as he can until he reaches the finish line.

A marathon is a long race. Marathon runners need just as much energy as sprinters do, but the way they expend it is very different. Success in the marathon depends on how effectively the runners pace themselves. All other factors being equal, the runner who knows when to speed up and when to slow down is far more likely to win—or even to finish the race at all.

The sprint strategy—run as fast as you can from beginning to end—can appear to be the only sensible approach to a race. It seems like you ought to be able to run a marathon as if it were a series of sprints—but it doesn't work that way. Part of the reason it doesn't work that way is the simple physical limit of human endurance. There's another factor here, too: To accommodate that limit, the marathon runner is constantly monitoring his own performance, watching for what's working and what isn't working, and adjusting his approach accordingly.

Web development is rarely a sprint. More often, there will be times when you push forward, building prototypes and generating ideas, followed by times when you pull back, testing what you've built, seeing how the pieces fit together, and refining the big picture for the project. Some tasks are best undertaken with an emphasis on speed; others require a more deliberate approach. Good marathon runners know which is which—so should you.

Thoughtful, deliberate design decisions will cost you time in the short term, but they will save you much more time in the long term. Designers and developers often lament the lack of attention to strategy, scope, and structure in the projects they work on. I have been involved in more than one project in which these activities were constantly under threat of being eliminated. Some people get impatient with tasks that don't involve the production of an actual site component like a graphic or a piece of code. These tasks are often the first line items cut from a project that's behind schedule or over budget.

But these tasks were included in the project scope in the first place because they served as essential preparation for later deliverables to come. When they are eliminated, the tasks and deliverables left in the project schedule feel uninformed by the larger context of the project, seeming disconnected from one another.

When you get to the end, you've got a product that falls short of everyone's expectations. Not only have you failed to solve your original problem, you've actually created new problems for yourself because now the next big project on the horizon is to attempt to address the shortcomings of the last project. And so the cycle repeats.

Looking at a site from the outside—or coming into the Web development process for the first time—it's easy to focus on the more obvious elements near the top of the five-plane model at the expense of those closer to the bottom. The irony, however, is that the elements that require close examination to perceive—the strategy, scope, and structure of the site—play a necessary role in the overall success or failure of the user experience.

Only by having someone in your organization think about each of the five planes can you address all the considerations crucial to creating a successful user experience. How these responsibilities are distributed in your organization isn't as important as making sure all the elements of user experience are accounted for.

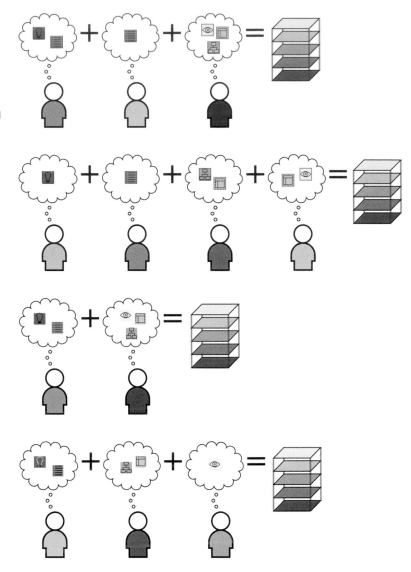

In many cases, failures on upper planes can obscure successes on lower planes. Problems with visual design—layouts that seem cluttered or busy, or colors that are inconsistent or clashing—can turn users off so quickly that they never discover all the smart choices you made with navigation or interaction design. Poorly conceived navigation design approaches can make all your work to create a sound, flexible information architecture seem like a waste of time.

Similarly, making all the right decisions on the upper planes means nothing if those decisions are founded on bad choices made on the lower planes. The history of the Web is strewn with sites that failed because, although they were beautiful, they were utterly unusable. Focusing on visual design to the exclusion of the other elements of user experience drove more than one startup into bankruptcy and led other companies to wonder why they were bothering with the Web at all.

It doesn't have to be that way. If you approach your Web development process with the complete user experience in mind, you can come out of it with a site that's an asset, not a liability. By making everything the user experiences on your site the result of a conscious, explicit decision, you can ensure that the site works to fulfill both your strategic goals and the needs of your users.

Index

Colophon

The Elements of User Experience was written and illustrated using Apple
PowerBook computers running Mac OS X. The text was composed with
BBEdit, organized with OmniOutliner, and edited with Microsoft Word.
Most of the illustrations were produced using OmniGraffle, some were cre-
ated in Adobe Illustrator, and some involved a bit of both. Screenshots were
produced through the magic of Command-Shift-3 and edited with Adobe
Photoshop.

This book was laid out in QuarkXPress. Body text was set in the Meridien
family; headings and captions were set in the Trade Gothic family. The book
was printed on 50# Husky Offset Smooth paper at R.R. Donnelley & Sons in
Crawfordsville, Indiana. Prepress consisted of PostScript computer-to-plate
technology (filmless process). The cover was printed on 12 pt. paper, coated
on one side, at Moore Langen Printing in Terre Haute, Indiana.

About jjg.net

"The Elements of User Experience" first debuted in March 2000 as a one-
page diagram on Jesse James Garrett's personal site: jjg.net. Since then, the
diagram has been downloaded by tens of thousands of Web designers and
developers around the world. Jesse's site also features one of the Web's most
popular compilations of resources for information architects and interaction
designers. The companion site for *The Elements of User Experience* includes
links to background material and additional resources on the topics covered
in the book.

http://www.jjg.net/elements/